D0821464

Testing African American Students

Special Re-Issue of
The Negro Educational Review

Editor
Asa G. Hilliard III

Third World Press
P.O. Box 19730
Chicago, IL 60619

Second Edition
First Printing 1995

ISBN: 0-88378-152-2 Paper

Manufactured in the United States of America

Cover design by Angelo Williams

Third World Press
P.O. Box 19730
Chicago, IL 60619

Special Issue of the Negro Educational Review
Testing African American Students

TABLE OF CONTENTS

Beyond the I.Q. Fiasco:
The Struggle for a Revolution in Professional Practice

The Testing of Black Students is Not a Trivial Matter

Josh Billings reportedly asserted, "it isn't ignorance that causes so much trouble; its what people know that isn't so." That seems to be precisely the case with the misguided notion that the voracious testing mania that is currently so pervasive in American education is the central mechanism in education reform in the United States of America. And yet, as competent educators have known for many years, and as the Educational Policies Commission pointed out a half century ago," "the supreme functions of the school is that of the teacher. Educational progress results from improved teaching, and in no other way whatsoever."[1]

Today the American people seem to be aghast and befuddled over the central purpose of education and the basic function of America's public schools. This confusion has created a void into which a dangerous combination of social ignorance, flagrant perambulation around the truth, and the widespread use of premises that seem plausible but are false has crept to effectively exploit and nurture the general public's lack of sophistication in fundamental matters concerning education and schools. This questionable development seems to have spawned and fostered the notion that the salvation of our nation and our schools requires that we concentrate on testing school children rather than on teaching them; on blaming and embarrassing school children for low test scores instead of teaching and nourishing them; on decapitating prospective teachers professionally by holding them up to public ridicule and scorn, before they can even begin their teaching careers, because of their test scores rather than encouraging them and teaching them how to teach children. The result has been the creation of an unfortunate climate of irrational confusion in which test scores are more likely to be used for exaggeration, flagellation, and titillation than for assessing and improving the teaching-learning process.

Nowhere is this dilemma of the prevailing irrational testing mania more brutal, mean and unhelpful than in the "Blacks score low on standardized tests" theme than has become a general rallying cry of many millions of white Americans, perhaps most of them, since May 17, 1954 and more specifically since the court decision in Swann vs. Charlotte-Mecklenburg

---

[1]Educational Policies Commission, *The Purposes of Education in American Democracy,* Washington, D.C., The National Education Association of the United States, 1938, p. 149.

County on April 21, 1971. What those who cherish this "Blacks score low on standardized tests" theme fail to add is that white America created and nourished the conditions responsible for these low test scores. The low test scores Black students make on standardized tests are ostensibly a function or a lack of intelligence. Moreover, it has been known for at least a half century that "when one controls the socio-economic cultural factors in a test...one finds sound statistical evidence that the average real intellectual ability [or what Binet calls 'capacity' as contrasted to 'information] is in general at the same level for all socio-economic groups."[2] Now, if we accept the theory that socio-economic factors influence one's performance on standardized tests significantly, it seems logical that we also accept the notion that the low scores Blacks make on these tests result to a very great extent from the fact that white racism has so thoroughly permeated the legacy of this nation that over the long sweep of its past an encrusted system of racial discrimination and segregation based on race has (a) deprived Black Americans of those experiences that cumulatively develop rich cultural backgrounds, (b) denied Black people those employment opportunities and associational outlets that enrich home life and social experience; (c) misdirected Black people's work habits, (d) instilled in a disturbingly large proportion of the nation's Black population a negative self-concept and a lack of self-confidence, and (e) distorted the school performance of Black students by a blatant failure to provide equal educational facilities for them or to ensure that the strength of the school's teaching programs were/are equally applied to Black and white enrollees.

Many school officials all around the country have "recently discovered" a huge gap in the test scores of Black and white pupils. As school superintendents and others periodically release reports to the public on how local [and even national] student test scores have risen, they emphasize that even though the scores of Black students have improved the disparity between Black and white student achievement scores persists — a trend they profess to find "profoundly disturbing." At the same time, many of them have bamboozled their communities, and a very large proportion of the American people, into believing that Black student test takers are responsible for the poor showing of American students on standardized tests such as the Scholastic Aptitude Test (SAT), without also stating that it has been primarily the performance of white students that has fallen off on the SAT.

---

[2]Allison Davis, "Socio-Economic Influences on Learning," *The Phi Delta Kappan*, January, 1957, p. 255.

[3]*Jacksonville Journal* (Florida), December 19, 1984, p. 5A; *The Washington Post*, September 11, 1985, p. A-14 and June 6, 1987, P. D-1; *Chicago Tribune*, October 4, 1986, Section 1, p. 10.

TABLE 1

Taking the S.A.T.: Black Scores Are Up

	Total		White		Black	
	Verbal	Math	Verbal	Math	Verbal	Math
1976	431	472	451	493	332	354
1977	429	470	448	489	330	357
1978	429	468	446	485	332	354
1979	427	467	444	483	330	358
1980	424	466	442	482	330	360
1981	424	466	442	483	332	362
1982	426	467	444	483	341	366
1983	425	468	443	484	339	369
1984	426	471	445	487	342	373
1985	431	475	N.A.	N.A.	N.A.	N.A.
1986	430	476	447	489	351	377
Change:	−.2%	+.8%	−.9%	−.8%	+5.8%	+6.5%

(1976 to 1986)   Source: College Board

For example, the data in Table 1 show clearly that the SAT scores of Black students rose significantly, while the SAT scores of white students hovered around the same level as in the latter years of the 1970s and actually declined during the eleven year period, 1976-1986. It seems not without significance to note more specifically that the data in Table 1 indicate that whereas the scores for white students on the verbal section of the SAT declined by 4 points or −9 per cent over the eleven-year period, the scores on the verbal section of the SAT for Black students rose by 19 points or +5.8 per cent. In like manner the data show that whereas the scores for white students on the mathematical section of the SAT declined over the eleven-year period by 4 points or −8 per cent, the scores on the mathematical section for Black students rose by 23 points or +6.5 per cent. Moreover, it is interesting to observe that not only have the SAT scores for Black students gone up at a higher rate than the scores for white students, but the scores of Black students have gone up at a higher rate than those of each of the other ethnic groups shown in Table 2.*

Table 2

SAT® Averages by Ethnic Group, 1976-1985

SAT-Verbal

	76*	77	78	79	80	81	82	83	84	85	% Change 1976-85
American Indian	388	390	387	386	390	391	388	388	390	392	+1.0
Asian-American	414	405	401	396	396	397	398	395	398	404	−2.3
Black	332	330	332	330	330	332	341	339	342	346	+4.2
Mexican-American	371	370	370	370	372	373	377	375	376	382	+3.0
Puerto Rican	364	355	349	345	350	353	360	358	358	368	+1.1
White	451	448	446	444	442	442	444	443	445	449	−0.4
Other	410	402	399	393	394	388	392	386	388	391	4.6
All Students	431	429	429	427	424	424	426	425	426	431	None

SAT-Mathematical

	76*	77	78	79	80	81	82	83	84	85	% Change 1976-85
American Indian	420	421	419	421	426	425	424	425	427	428	+1.9
Asian-American	518	514	510	511	509	513	513	514	519	518	None
Black	354	357	354	358	360	362	366	369	373	376	+6.2
Mexican-American	410	408	402	410	413	415	416	417	420	426	+3.9
Puerto Rican	401	397	388	388	394	398	403	403	405	409	+2.0
White	493	489	485	483	482	483	483	484	487	491	−.04
Other	458	457	450	447	449	447	449	446	450	448	−2.2
All Students	472	470	468	467	466	466	467	468	471	475	+.06

*1976 is the first year for which SAT scores by ethnic group are available.

In observing the SAT scores for Black students in both Tables 1 and 2, even if one assumes that variations of 2, 3, or 4 points per year are not important, long-term gains are. So as one looks back over the eleven-year period, 1976-87, and observes consistent growth in the scores of Black students, that is a good omen. It is the steady progression shown in the SAT scores of Black students that is important. Further observation of the data presented in Table 2 shows that whereas the SAT scores of other minority group students have gone up steadily in recent years their increases have not been as large as those in the scores of Black students, but have generally exceeded the increases in the scores of white students.

Whereas few would deny that continued improvement in the test scores of Black students (and all other students) on standardized tests is a desirable goal, the facts presented in this discussion make it legitimate to ask why the high priority of so many school systems throughout the United States is reportedly centered around boosting test scores, especially those of Black students, through a host of stagnating attempts to be innovative rather than through good teaching of high quality. Verily, when all expressions of alarm over the benighted state of test performance of students, and especially Black students, and of the serious and sincere intent to bring about a meaningful measure of improvement in same are finished, the irrefutable truth remains that "there is no procedure that can render substance unnecessary, there is no technique of classroom ledgerdemain that can take the place of scholarly competence."[4]

The foregoing presentation seems to indicate that test scores are neither measures of racial characteristics nor of the cumulative skills a student has acquired during school experience; that test scores neither measure the quality of our schools nor either the real or most important competencies needed to function effectively in our society. In the final analysis, are test scores merely mirrors that reflect the socio-economic milieu that has conditioned the test-takers lives and lay out the dimensions of societal problems to be solved. or is Michael Kinsley[5] correct when he asserts that "the real social function of the SAT is as the central affirmation of American meritocracy. It justifies the pecking order and reminds people that they deserve their place in it." After all, "it isn't ignorance that causes so much trouble; its what people know that isn't so."

— R. Grann Lloyd

---

[4]American Historical Association, Report of the Commission on the Social Studies, *Conclusions and Recommendations of the Commission*, New York, New York: Charles Scribner's Sons, 1934, pp. 71-72.

[5]*The Wall Street Journal*, "SATs are a) Flawed, b) Comical, c) Both of the Above," September 4, 1986, p. 27.

*Issued as a news release by the College Board on September 23, 1985. Percent changes were added by the writer.

Guest Editor

Dr. Asa G. Hilliard, III

Dr. Asa G. Hilliard III, an educational psychologist, and historian has been a teacher, researcher, school administrator, and professional writer for many years. He has specialized in the study of psychological test validity in cross cultural usage, child development, improved teaching methods, and Ancient African History — especially Ancient Kemetic (Egyptian) history.

Dr. Hilliard has been prominent as an expert witness in litigation on test validity for African Americans. He serves as a member of the American Psychological Association Committee of Psychological Tests and Assessment. He is a founding member of the Association for the Study of Classical African Civilization and serves as its 2nd vice president.

Professor Hilliard served for eight years as Dean of Education at San Francisco State University before joining the faculty at Georgia State University as Fuller E. Callaway Professor of Education. He has presented numerous guest lectures at major universities throughout the United States. Dr. Hilliard has also served and studied internationally in such countries as Liberia, Egypt, Nigeria, Uganda, Tanzania, Kenya, Guam, Samoa, Suriname, the Virgin Islands, England, Greece and other European countries.

Dr. Hilliard has received many awards for his work. Among them are the following:

Outstanding Scholarship Award, National Association of Black Psychologists

Marcus M. Foster Distinguished Educator Award, National Alliance of Black School Educators

M. L. K., Jr. award for outstanding research, scholarly achievement and humanitarian service, New York Society of Clinical Psychologists

Distinguished Leadership Award, National Association of Teacher Educators

Introduction

by
Asa G. Hilliard III

In 1977 the late Dr. Norman Dixon, a close friend and a gifted educator was given the task of producing a special issue of the Negro Educational Review (NER). The subject of the issue was standardized testing as it affected African Americans. It proved to be one of the most popular issues of the NER ever. That issue spoke to an urgent need, the need to expose the widespread abuses of standardized testing and in education with African American populations. Years later that need still exists. If anything, the uses of standardized testing have expanded and abuses have become even more acute. As a result the Editor and Board of the NER have called for a sequel to that issue.

I.Q. testing, developmental inventories, minimum competency testing of students and teachers, aptitude testing, employment testing for certification, hiring, promotions and retentions, personality testing, interest inventories, and polygraph testing are but a few of the uses of standardized paper and pencil, mostly multiple choice tests and other devices. When we see a dramatic decline in the number of African American teachers, a dramatic decline in the number of African American students in colleges and universities, a dramatic reduction in the number of teachers being prepared at Black colleges, and a continuing disproportion in the numbers of African American children in special education classes, standardized testing seems to play a key role. Therefore, we have a special interest in assuring that testing instruments and practices are valid measures for African Americans.

These matters before us are parts of a complex whole, a whole that is too great to cover in any comprehensive way here. Matters that concern us involved **educational philosophy, educational and psychological theory, psychometric theory and practice** and **educational utility**. Ultimately a complete understanding of issues and practices will require the contribution of a multidisciplinary group of scholars in such fields as sociology, psychology, education, cultural linguistics, anthropology and even political science. We make the attempt here to present articles by a multidisciplinary group of scholars who, collectively, bring unique perspectives on the matter of standardized testing in education and in education related areas. Their work gives a glimpse of what must be done. In some cases, original lines of inquiry, research and analysis are evident.

One thing is certain. It is not enough in our critique to argue that present test developers and users often do not follow their own stated rules or that their work is incomplete. At certain points it is the rules that must be questioned as inappropriate, since invalid assumptions, paradigms, and constructs are often used in making up the system of rules for test making. For example, the assumption that human intellect is fixed has led to the use of I.Q. tests to measure the presumed static mental condition, when cognition is clearly dynamic. Even more problematic is the fact that virtually no one in psychometry today questions the bedrock assumption that language data can be used for scientific measurement, especially in a society and world that is characterized by linguistic pluralism. The noted sociolinguist Roger Shuy has made some startling statements in an old manuscript (1975) entitled "Quantitative linguistic data: A case for and some warnings against".

> "Meanwhile it will do for us to examine some recent uses of quantitative language analyses from the perspective of the linguist. As noted earlier, linguists generally feel more comfortable about using quantitative analyses to probe for patterned differences than to generalize for broad groupings. **Likewise, the more linguists study the semantic and pragmatic meaning conveyed by language, the less comfortable they become about the possibility of accurate measurement of tests which use language as a medium. It is beginning to be believed, in fact, that the most critical measurement points of all, at least as far as language is concerned, are the ones least susceptible to quantification.**
>
> A basic problem is that the goal of getting responses that will be comparable across subjects or across testing times is often realized by forcing one standard interpretation of a question (or stimulus) and answer (or response) that is, in fact, not uniquely interpretable but rather is vague and can be fully specified only with reference to specifics of the individual test-takers' background and the individual test-taking occasion."

Naturally the psychometric community is either ignorant of the findings of such scientists, or they choose deliberately to ignore them. Until such time as psychometrists deal with such matters as these, they must be regarded as something other than scientists.

Collected here in one place is a set of articles that raise many issues, only some of which are now a part of the professional dialogue on the design and use of standardized tests and assessment. The value of having these writings together in one place is that we can see some of the major gaps in professional theory and practice. There is a kind of academic monopoly in testing that determines the topics that get attention. As a result, criticisms from African American scientists and others, who have too little power to influence the choice of topics, are usually interpreted as demands for "fairness". By labeling such concerns merely as "fairness" concerns, it leaves the impression that only mainstream Eurocentric academic opinion stands on "scientific" ground. Therefore responses to criticism from African American scientists and others are treated after the "scientific" issues have been decided, if they are treated at all.

The articles presented here are selected to present challenges to the theoretical and applied science of standardized testing and assessment. The straightest pathway to "fairness" is scientific validity. With scientific validity no special pleas need be made regarding such things as adjustments for "minorities" in cut off scores or special admissions to openings in classes for the "gifted".

A special feature of this issue is that we introduce the concept and orientation of African Psychology and its application in testing and assessment. African Psychology is an approach to science that is rooted in assumptions, constructs and paradigms that flow from the cultural reality of people of African descent. This approach was formalized initially during the late 1960's. Prominent among the seminal thinkers in this vital area were Dr. Wade Nobles, Dr. Cedric X, Dr. Phil McGee and Dr. Naim Akbar. All have continued to develop the field and are now joined by many other psychologists.

European Psychology also exists without a label and prefers to conceive of itself as universal. For the most part, academic narcissism on the part of these psychologists has caused them to confine their attention to their own views. They have failed to respond to the challenge of African psychology.

We provide in a section of this issue several articles that reflect an African centered approach.

For example, Dr. Wade Nobles offers an analysis that proceeds from a knowledge of African American history and culture; and a set of basic assumptions that differ radically from what appears in mainstream professional psychology. His brilliant observations cannot be summarily dismissed. Search the pages of mainstream psychometric literature and one will find no serious and competent response to Dr. Nobles. Likewise Dr. Joseph Baldwin presents original insights on assessment issues from an African centered perspective. Ultimately to be valid, assessment of African Americans must benefit from the seminal thought of such scholars as Drs. Nobles and Baldwin.

There are two primary aspects of the experience of African Americans that call for a modification of traditional practice in assessment. On the one hand, there is an African culture and an African American culture. People of African or African American descent are immersed in the culture to a greater or lesser degree. Mental capacities or functions, operations, and structures are expressed only through specific cultural material that is familiar to the testee. Therefore assessment must account for cultural realities if it is to be scientific. Second, African Americans (and Africans in other parts of the world) have had special experiences with oppression. The domination/oppression equation operates by certain rules and yields certain consequences in the behavior of oppressor and oppressed that are unrelated to abilities. Assessment practice in general fails to account for the functioning of systems of oppression. For example, in personality assessment we may see that clients from oppressed groups may fail to disclose their feelings to therapists from dominant groups. Likewise the dominance/oppression equation may curtail motivations and affect the self-image of learners. These are realities that must be accounted for in assessment practice. At present, they are not even acknowledged, not to mention explained.

Dr. Orlando Taylor, world renowned linguist and his colleague Dr. Dorian Lee have tackled the problem of measurement with linguistic data. Grounded in African American culture they, like Dr. Mary Hoover and Dr. Alice Scales provide the theoretical and empirical basis for an appropriate interpretation of language based tests. A close reading of their work suggests directions for the future in psychometrics.

Mr. John Weiss and Dr. Beverly Cole have written articles on the important matter of the impact of standardized testing on client populations. Mr. Weiss does a beautiful job of untangling the twisted web of activity in testing. Dr. Cole provides the data to show how coaching would help African American children, **if**, they had equal access to it as compared to affluent European Americans.

We are fortunate to be in a unique position to include in this issue three case reports from large urban school districts. These case studies all involve responses to issues associated with I.Q. testing that have been litigated. All seek either to eliminate I.Q. testing with African American children or to modify their use. In each case an attempt has been made to use new assessment approaches that seek to link testing and instruction. Dr. Harold Dent in San Francisco, Dr. Pat Heaston in Chicago and Mrs. Ingrid Draper, Mrs. Aleatha Hamilton and Mrs. Janet Jones in Detroit provide us with a rare in-depth glimpse of what it means to try to modify professional practices for the benefit of children. Nowhere else is there likely to be three situations that are so comparable. We are fortunate that they could be reported here. Preceding the case studies and following them are articles by Dr. Asa Hilliard, III that set forth certain basic issues associated with I.Q. type mental measurement. He also writes about the Dynamic Assessment alternative to I.Q. that stimulated the work that is being done in San Francisco, Chicago, and Detroit. Finally the full text of the Ninth Circuit Federal Court of Appeals ruling on the use of I.Q. tests with African American children is included. This appeal of Larry P. vs. Wilson Riles ruling was just decided in the fall of 1986. It is a remarkable ruling. It should be reviewed in detail.

This special issue concludes with two excellent reviews of two important books. Dr. Al McWilliams and Dr. Shirley Biggs do crisp and penetrating critiques that should pique the interest of a broad range of professionals.

AFRICAN CULTURE AND
PSYCHOLOGICAL ASSESSMENT:

Theory and Practice

Psychometrics and African-American Reality: A Question of Cultural Antimony

by
Wade W. Nobles

The problem of psychological assessment has been the historical arena where controversy and criticism has surfaced as the cutting edge issue relative to the African-American community. From the use of the MMPI to evaluate Black men and women in this country's prisons to the use of I.Q. tests to place Black children in EMR classes to the use of various aptitude tests as "gate keepers" to future access and opportunity, psychometry has been an area of fundamental concern. The overarching issue of what is mental functioning and how it is assessed is, in fact, problematic. Grossman[1] has stated in this regard that the factors which determine mental retardation for instance are developmental lags in intellectual functioning, personal independence and social responsibility. As such, mental retardation is defined as "the condition which exists when there is significantly sub-average general intellectual functioning concurrent with deficits in adaptive behavior". Adaptive behavior, in turn, is defined as "the effectiveness, in degree, with which the individual meets the standards of personal independence and social responsibility expected of one's age and cultural group". Retarded mental functioning would, therefore, be a condition where one possesses sub-average intelligence and fails to meet the cultural expectations of one's group. Psychometrically, the determination of mental retardation would be to measure both one's intelligence and attainment of cultural expectations. How does one however measure the attainment of cultural expectations? For that matter, how does one measure intelligence? The failure to do the latter, (fairly or objectively), in fact, is the major point of confrontation between the discipline of Black Psychology and Western Psychology. The essential point of contention (cf: Hilliard[2]; Kamin[3]; BAABP,[4]) in this confrontation

---

[1]Grossman, H.J. (ed) *Manual on Terminology and Classification in Mental Retardation.* American Association on Mental Deficiency, (Special Publication No. 2) Washington, D.C. 1977.

[2]Hilliard, Asa G., III. "Alternatives to I.Q. Testing: An Approach to the Identification of 'Gifted' Minority Children." *Final Report.* California State Department of Education, Special Education Support Unit. Eric Clearinghouse of Early Childhood Education, 146-009, 1976.

[3]Kamin, Leon J. *The Science of Politics of I.Q.* Potomac, Maryland: Lawrence Erlbaum Associates, 1979.

[4]Bay Area Association of Black Psychologists. "Position Statement on the Use of I.Q. and Ability Tests" in Reginald Jones (ed) *Black Psychology.* Harper & Row Publishers, New York, 1972.

was the recognition and/or denial (depending on which group one finds oneself) that intelligence testing was culture bound and cannot in its natural content and form adequately assess the intelligence of African-American people. The problem, of course, is that psychometry itself is culture bound. The field of mental measurement was in part developed and propagated by people committed to a particular social world view and cultural orientation. Psychometry is not the objective and systematic assessment of various mental dispositions and/or attitudes. Psychometry is a "mega-business complex" bringing together the interest of racist science and capitalist commercial interests. The problem with psychometry is actually found in both its historical development and its contemporary practice.

Psychometry and Western Consciousness

The assault on African people by the misuse of tools of psychometry and racist scientific theories is long standing. As early as the turn of the century, white psychologists and educators were amassing their psychometric armaments to justify the continued oppression of African-American people.

The prevailing intellectual atmosphere was and is shaped by racist thinking and assumptions. In 1956, for example, the prestigious literary magazine, "Putnam's Monthly" published the common thinking of the time wherein an anonymous author noted that,

> "the most minute and the most careful researchers have as yet, failed to discover a history or any knowledge of ancient times among the negro races. They have invented no writing; not even the crude picture-writing of the lowest tribes; they have no gods and no heroes; no epic poems and no legend, not even simple traditions. There never existed among them an organized government; they never ruled a hierarchy or an established church".[5]

This unidentified author goes on to conclude in his argument that the few evidences of African splendor or civilization were borrowed from Europe; and that where there is an African religion or creed or knowledge, customs and progress, they too came from outside of Africa. The African in effect has no history and makes no history. Three decades later, Harvard University's William McDougall indicated from his Ivy league citadel that "a policy of segregation of the colored people of the United States is the only sound one".

The establishment of the inferiority of African and African-American peoples via psychometry assessment immediately replaced the shallow pseudo-religious theories of pre-destiny and Divine curse. The most interest-

---

[5]Putnam's Monthly, "Uncle Tom at Home" (anonymous contributor) Vol. VIII, No. XLIII, July, 1956, pp 4-5.

ing case of this psychometric propaganda occurred shortly after the 1954 Brown vs. Board of Education decision. In 1958, Profesor Audrey M. Shuey at Randolph-Macon College in Virginia published *The Testing of Negro Intelligence* (Shuey, 1958) wherein she reviewed over three hundred original investigations of negro intelligence conducted during the previous five decades. Professor Shuey's intention or purpose as noted by Chase (1980) was to interpret the prevailing psychometric wisdom so as to substantiate her belief (offered as a conclusion) that those mental test scores "all taken together, inevitably point to the presences of native differences between Negroes and Whites as determined by intelligence tests" (pp. 521). Parenthetically, the White Citizens Council in addition to distributing (for the cost of $1.00) dozens of so-called scientific pamphlets and bulletins on race and racial problems (particularly Henry E. Carretts', "Race and Psychology"; "Heredity: The Cause of Racial Differences in Intelligence" and "The Relative Intelligence of Whites and Negroes"), the council also distributed Shuey's work. It should also be noted that Dr. Garrett was the chairman of the Department of Psychology at Columbia University and served consecutive terms as the president of **The Psychometric Society**, the Eastern Psychological Association and the American Psychological Association. Garrett waged his psychometric war on African-American people from the halls of the American Psychological Association to the shores of the Patrick Henry Press. Through this latter publication, Garrett's psychometric propaganda was printed in enormous editions (i.e. 200,000 copies of a 26' page pamphlet on classroom desegregation plus 85,000 copies of the second printing) and purposely distributed to newspaper editors and columnists, teachers, preachers, politicians and "influential citizens" in all of the fifty states. A similar example of psychometric warfare was the publication of Carleton Putnam's, "Race and Reason",[6] which again documented the low I.Q. scores of Blacks as well as our low income and high crime rates.

The Louisiana State Board of Education purchased 5,000 copies of Race and Reason for use in the schools of Louisiana and a self-appointed group of influential "southern gentlemen" organized the Putnam letters committee to pay for the distribution of the writings, teachings and open letters of Carleton Putnam about the race problem.

It should be noted that the Society for the Psychological Study of Social Issues (SPSSI) openly opposed this type of scientific racism and psychometric warfare. In addition to its 1961 resolution attacking such "scholarship", it also sponsored APA member books with a counter perspective on the

---

[6]Putnam, Carleton, *Race and Reason: A Yankee View*. Washington, D.C.: Public Affairs Press, 1961.

problems of race, education and society. One of the most important volumes of this effort was the text, *Social Class, Race and Psychological Development* edited by Martin Deutsch, Irwin Katz and Arthur Jensen[7], wherein basic scientific data was offered to support the notion that socio-economic and/or environmental causes were the antecedent to differential learning capacity of the poor and non-poor, Black children and White children. Eight years later, however, one of the above mentioned scholars, Arthur Jensen[8], openly recanted the "error of his ways" and published in the prestigious Harvard Education Review his new found born-again belief or conviction that at least 80% of the intellectual development of human beings is controlled by the genes they inherit from their parents and that as a unitary trait, intelligence can be measured accurately with I.Q. tests. This born-again psychometric warrior further noted that not only is intelligence at least 80% genetic, but that the different races differ in their racial intelligence quotients.

In this regard, he notes in his book, *Educability and Group Differences*[9] that the possibility of a biochemical connection between skin pigmentation and intelligence is not unlikely in view of the biological relation between melanin and some of the neurotransmitter substances in the brain. In effect, Black skin is related to Black brains which have been psychometrically proven to be inferior to white brains. In addition to Jensen, several highly placed "generals", (Harvard University Professor Richard Hornstein; Stanford University Physics Professor William Shockley[10]), of the psychometric wars emerged and gained national prominence and attention.

The evidence for an undeclared psychometric war on African-Americans is rather clearly explained in Allan Chase's[11] *The Legacy of Malthus*. It is not, however, our task to review this record. The psychological war against African-Americans has been fairly well documented (i.e. Hilliard[12]; Nobles[13];

---

[7]Deutsch, M., I. Katz and A.R. Jensen (eds). *Social Class, Race and Psychological Development*. New York: Holt, Rhinehart and Winston, Inc. 1968.

[8]Jensen, Arthur. "How Much Can We Boost I.Q. and Scholastic Achievement", *Harvard Educational Review*, 39 (1), 1969.

[9]Jensen, Arthur. *Educability and Group Differences*. New York: Harper & Row, 1973.

[10]Shuey, Audrey M. *The Testing of Negro Intelligence*. 2nd ed,; New York: Social Science Press, 1966.

[11]Chase, Allan. *The Legacy of Malthus: The Social Cost of The New Scientific Racism.* University of Illinois Press, Chicago, 1980.

[12]Hilliard, Asa G. III. "I.Q. Thinking as the Emperor's New Clothes: A Critique of Jensen's Bias in Mental Testing" in Cecil Reynolds (ed). *Perspectives on Bias in Mental Testing.* Plenum Press, 1982.

[13]Nobles, Wade W., et al. "Critical Analysis of Scholarship on Black Family Life", United Church of Christ Commission for Racial Justice, *Final Report*, Washington, D.C. 1983.

Guthrie[14]). The ultimate question is why?: Why in relation to African people does science become racist and its tools (i.e. psychometry) weapons?

The answer it seems is found in the historical clash of cultures. If one examines, for instance, the historical contact between Africa and the West, the one outstanding sign having special meaning was the invention of "the Negro". It is extremely important to recognize the concept and meaning of "The Negro" is an entirely different and distinct ideological construct from the image and meaning of the African which proceeded its (the concept of the Negro) inclusion into European consciousness. There is no stretching of the point to note that literally from the beginning of human consciousness to the advent of "the Negro", the relationship between the African and the European had been the opposite of what it is now. The contact between cultures began long before the events of the 15th and 16th century which set into motion the ultimate domination and control of Africa. With the exception of a few minor interruptions Black people or the Africans were feared and respected by Whites or European people. The meaning of the Africans in their (the whites) historical consciousness was associated with high culture, superior civilizations and sophisticated human systems of organization (i.e., law, commerce, family, etc).

From the time of the Ionian philosophers, to the Roman Ascension to the Moorish conquest of the Iberian peninsula, evidence abounds that the Europeans viewed the Blacks with awe and respect. The terms Ethiop, Blackamoor, Nubian and African all represented, in the minds of the European, a culture and people who were superior, dominant and their antagon. The psychological requisite for European domination was therefore the destruction of African civilization and the re-definition of the African. These two conditions are, in fact, the necessary and sufficient condition for European world domination. The European, in effect, had to re-define the African so that we differed in mentality, attitude, function (behavior) and belief from that which allowed us to rule the known world and shape the process of human development. Enter here on the stage of human history the necessity for inventing the concept of "Negro" and the permanent installation of a Judeo-Christian Greco-Roman ideological bases of Western civilization. With the establishment of philosophical doctrines of domination and exploitation like the "Imperium Christianum", "Regnum Europae" or "Societas Christianum", Europe emerged from the Dark Ages committed to a new interpretation of history and human consciousness steeped thoroughly and inextricably in Eurocentrism. The requisite condition for the legitimacy of this Eurocentrism was the destruction of the Afro-centric World and the

---

[14]Guthrie, Robert V. *Even the Rat was White*. Harper & Row Publishers, New York, 1976.

establishment of the human construct known as "The Negro". Having invented "The Negro", European ascension required that it (the Negro) have meaning which proved European superiority. Hence, the adoption of the belief in the inferiority of African people as the guiding perspective of all Western scholarships as pertaining to the African, now re-classified as the Negro. The ultimate proof of European superiority was, of course, not subjective opinion or personal desire but "scientific fact". It is at this point, as mentioned above, that the queen discipline of human understanding, (i.e. psychology) becomes racist and it's tools of mental measurement (i.e. psychometry) as instrument of falsification, domination and exploitation.

Psychometrics, Paradigms and Paradox: The Question of Cultural Antimony

It is indeed unfortunate that the advent of the disciplines devoted to the study of human development (i.e., psychology, anthropology, etc.) paralleled the establishment of Eurocentricism as a world order. As a consequence of this co-terminal development, the question of what is authentic culture and how do we understand and assess the human experience of other people has undergone continuous confusion, debate and criticism.

The way in which a people view the world or universe is critical, if not fundamental, to all the life-space activities they engage in. A people's conceptual universe not only determines their human capacities (e.g. intelligence), it also guides the development of any new human "inventions". How we define and classify both regular and irregular patterns of social interaction, behavior and development is consequently determined and guided by our conceptual universe. In fact, one could go so far as to say that the meaning of human (social) relationships is both defined and determined by one's conceptual universe.

In terms of science the conceptual universe takes the form of a "paradigm". Technically, this paradigm serves as a formalized framework which guides the assessment and evaluation of reality. At the heart of this issue is the fact that the notion of a conceptual universe has implied in it a more central set of ideas. The centricity (i.e., Eurocentrism) of the conceptual universe gives it a particular focus and/or orientation.

Given the necessities of European world domination it is appropriate to re-note that the central set of ideas in the Eurocentric conceptual universe is the "wished for" and "imagined" inferiority of African people. Accordingly, when the Eurocentric conceptual universe takes the form of a scientific paradigm and serves thereby as an instrument for "knowing" there is a fundamental flaw in its allegiance to the requirement of scientific objectivity as pertaining to non-European people. Parenthetically, it should also be noted that as paradigms are replaced, or more accurately, as the centrality of a particular conceptual universe shifts to a different or new set of ideas, how we define and classify patterns of social interaction and human development, including mental measurement, also change.

In the history of the natural sciences one can best find examples of shifts on the central set of ideas which support a particular conceptual universe. For instance, the change from Ptolemaic to Copernican celestial science really represented a paradigmatic shift in conceptualization. Likewise the reconceptualization of mechanical rebounding to electro-static repulsion is a similar shift in the way of "knowing". These changes in paradigm, accordingly, represent a change in the way one conceives/perceives his universe.

What should be apparent, here, is that in the universe of people, our contemporary world has been viewed as Euro-centered. By that, it is simply meant that the core set of ideas viewed as legitimately representing the human condition were (are) based on a European "view" of the universe. This Euro-centrism thus served as the paradigm for knowing. Since the 15th century, the Euro-centric paradigm, accordingly, has been used to define and classify social interaction and human development. Hence, most, if not all, standards of human behavior and understanding are shaped by this Euro-centric paradigm.

The paradigm, indeed influences and shapes all aspects of the scientific enterprise, including its conceptualizations, methodology and techniques. The more general category of cross-cultural research techniques, for example, utilizes various methods and techniques to test hypotheses about human behavior amongst various peoples throughout the world. The application of cross-cultural methods is supposedly to ensure that one's findings relate to human behavior in general and not just to behavior of a single culture. In effect, the intent of cross-cultural research is to "discover" the universality of human behavior.

When one, however, examines the application of racial and comparative research as examples of cross-cultural research an interesting phenomenon occurs. For the most part, racial and comparative research (especially psychometric comparisons) with African-American populations don't explore the "universality" of behavior. Instead, there is the assumption of the innate inferiority of African people. In fact, one can argue that the racial and comparative method in psychometry rather than test the "theory" of Black intellectual inferiority, actually defends and protects the theory from refutation[15].

The problems associated with cross-cultural research are found in the notion of the "equivalence of culture" which in turn raises questions regarding the "equivalence of meaning", for the variables, subject status, conceptualization, measurements, sampling, analyses and interpretation. If the meaning (and experience) of intelligence, for instance, differs between two cultures then the results of the psychometric assessment of intelligence would in fact be meaningless.

According to Whiting, the acquisition of meaningful information in cross-cultural research depends on the researcher's ability to maximize cultural homogeneity within one's definition of study case. He argues in this regard that to ensure that the local community units are reasonably equivalent with respect to homogeneity, they should ideally have features which serve to reduce the variability of both individual behavior and the cultural beliefs, values and techniques held by the community members. Accordingly, he suggests that comparative units should have the following factors: (1) members have frequent face-to-face contact with one another; (2) they speak the same dialect; (3) they have some degree of sovereignty; and (4) they have a group name.

There are of course two problems with Whiting's criterion for cross-cultural research. The primary and most important flaw is that this strategy is designed so as to minimize cultural differences. The explication of cultural differences for the purpose of establishing universals is really the only valid reason for doing cross-cultural research. Unless of course one is doing mono-cultural research with the intent of demonstrating how deviant one culture is from another (standard) culture. This is not cross-cultural research. The second flaw is that the criteria are really designed to maximize "between" cultural homogeneity. It doesn't, therefore, address the problem of conceptual equivalence between two distinct cultural groups. If one could, nevertheless, identify a culturally homogeneous Black and White group utilizing Whiting's criteria, one would still have remaining, the problem of "stimuli relevance", "comparability of response" and "differential meanings".

Consistent with Whiting's notion, in psychometric assessment the task is, therefore, to maximize cultural homogeneity by minimizing the importance and integrity of race. This occurs most often by classifying race as a "status variable" whose importance in the research process is that status

[15]Banks, Curtis W. "Deconstructive Falsification: Foundations of Critical Method in Black Psychology" in Enrico Jones & Sheldon Korchin (eds.), *Minority Mental Health*, New York; Peneger Press, 1982.

variables need to be controlled, randomized or held constant so that their effects are neutralized, cancelled out or equated for all conditions[16].

The essential crises of psychometry, of course, is found in the difficulty it has in appropriately defining human intelligence or mental attitudes which are consistent with the cultural meanings of both human communities. It is, therefore, within the realm of culture, that the crises and critical flaw of racial and comparative research, particularly psychometric assessment is found.

In recognition, therefore, that the goal of science is to "understand" and not singularly or only to predict and control phenomena, the task of scientific inquiry is to ultimately establish general laws about human phenomena, which, in turn, serve as instruments for systematic explanation, and provide the basis for dependable prediction. Scientific inquiry and method are, nevertheless, idiosyncratic to a people's cultural deep structure.

In effect, the program in psychometrics is that rather than establish the universality of mental functioning between Black and White people; it, by its very nature, denies the cultural integrity of Black people and thereby fails to explicate the binding cultural laws within each group which is the basis of human mental functioning and which may serve as the key to understanding the universality of human mentalities.

Racial and comparative methods, as currently utilized, are idiosyncratic to the laws and assumptions of primarily Euro-American culture. Hence, if we are to elevate the assessment of Black mental functioning to more than a "tinted reflection" of White mental functioning we must start with a theoretical and empirical framework which is capable of reducing the elements of Black reality into intellectually manageable properties without compromising the historical truths and cultural principles of African and African-American people.

A Paradox is a statement or tenet which is discordant with what is held to be established belief. Scientific Paradox would, therefore, be those conceptualizations, data and findings which are contrary to established opinion and belief. Even when or especially when the belief or opinion are unstated. Antimony is a contradiction in a law or a contradiction between two binding laws[17]. Culture, as the process which gives a people a general design for living and patterns for interpreting their reality, implies that there

---

[16]Issac, Stephen and Michael B. William. *Handbook in Research and Evaluation*, Edits Publishers, San Diego, 1971.

[17]Nobles, Wade W. "Paradym, Paradox and Power: The Dilemma of States in Racial and Comparative Research", Paper presented to the Institute for Urban Affairs and Research, Conference on Racial and Comparative Research, Howard University, Washington, D.C., Oct. 17 &18, 1985.

are cultural laws (guiding principles) which are consistent with the requirements of the people's cultural deep structure. Accordingly, the "cultural
laws" of two different groups can and often are in contradistinction. When
the cultural substance or deep structure between two or more cultures stands
in contradistinction of each other, it can result in contradiction in their
respective meanings of reality. This contradiction of meaning results in a
state of "Cultural Antimony".

In effect, the Eurocentric cultural paradigm or the Eurocentric formalized
framework which guides the assessment and evaluation of reality stands in
contradistinction of the cultural laws which are consistent with the cultural
deep structure of African people. The specific cultural Antimony (i.e.,
contradiction in law or between two laws) is in the assumed white superiority. Keep in mind that up until the 15th century, the cultural law, embedded
in the historical consciousness of European people, was the acceptance of
African grandeur and superiority. The advent of the construct "Negro" with
all its connotations of inferiority, savagery, unholy and uncivilized represents in fact and deed a contradiction in the European historical consciousness.

The Euro-American belief (now presented as objective scientific findings) about African and African-American "inferiority" stands in contradistinction with the belief about African "superiority" which is found in
European historical consciousness. The fact that the European community
set about to develop scientific theories about Black inferiority and methods
(i.e. psychometry) to defend those theories from repetition does not change
the state of antimony.

The technical criticism of psychometry has ranged from issues and
concerns involving (1) the misuse (or more properly, the political use) of
testing; (2) the technical weakness associated with test reliability, objectivity, validity and standardization; (3) the guiding assumption of test construction models (i.e., deficit vs. difference, heterogeneity vs. homogeneity); and
(4) the educational, legal and economic implications/applications of test
data. Each and every one of these concerns points to serious problems in
psychometry. The source of these problems, however, lie in or can be traced
to the perceived necessity to verify the falsification of the historical presence
and position of African people in relation to Europeans. Cultural antimony,
understandably, complicates the comprehension of the problem. With the
continued uncritical use of psychometric methods and theories one can, in
effect, make the phenomena equal to what the test is capable of measuring
about the phenomena. By this is meant, that without knowing the meaning
given to mental functioning which is consistent with the cultural laws of
African and African-American reality, one can mistakenly settle for or
accept a meaning of African-American mental functioning which is only that

which is taped or measured by the existing psychometric instrumentation and/or techniques. Hence, or accordingly, the tools of psychometrics can become the ultimate instrument for delimiting the meaning and definition of African and African-American mental functioning.

It will be critical for the field of mental measurement that as African-American scholars as well as the better trained Euro-American scholars engage in the continued debate surrounding psychometry and African-American reality that we understand that the real source of the problem is to be found in the historical "clash of minds" and confrontation between African and European cultures. If, in effect, psychometry is to become a tool of mental measurement which assesses the universality of mental functioning (which parenthetically, given the centrality of culture in determining human meaning may be an impossibility) then the field psychometry must free itself from the legacy of the subtle and sublime as well as the overt and intentional European obsession with justifying its own superiority.

African Psychology and Black Personality Testing

by
Joseph A. Baldwin

INTRODUCTION

The recently developing Black personality paradigm in African (Black) Psychology has generated a major breakthrough in Black personality assessment. Over the past two decades, perhaps the most significant development in African Psychology has been the fuller clarification and articulation of the **African worldview** as the philosophical-conceptual framework for conceptualizing African-American experience and the African-American personality. This in turn has provided for the generation of the appropriate cultural specific or "Africentric" assessment strategies and instrumentation for use in the study of the Black personality, and having significant implications for the diagnosis and treatment of Black mental health problems. Before engaging in a more specific discussion of the critical issues involved in these recent developments in African Psychology, a brief examination of some of the earlier activities surrounding Black personality assessment will help to lay the historical context for a discussion of contemporary trends in this area.

While the formal development of African psychology (by Black psychologists) in Western society is only a little over two to three decades old,[1] numerous attempts at Black personality assessment outside of this framework have been undertakened.[2] These earlier attempts at assessment, virtually without exception, were essentially "oppression-centered" or victim analyses, and generated a variety of obscure and often racist constructs and interpretations, or more accurately stated, **misrepresentations** of the Black personality. These models viewed the Black personality as not only essentially reactive in nature, but also as motivated in terms of a purely negatively based psychological energy. In other words, the Black personality was conceptualized as the net result of the forces of Euro-American racial oppression rather than cultural affirmative forces. Thus, a fundamental problem or limitation of these earlier "Non-Africentric" approaches to

---

[1] J.A. Baldwin, "Black psychology and Black personality." *Black Books Bulletin*, IV (1976), 6-11, 65. J.Q. Baldwin, "African (Black) Psychology: Issues and synthesis," *Journal of Black Studies*, XVI (1986), 235-249. G.G. Jackson, "The origin and development of Black psychology," *Studia Africana*, I (1979), 279-293. G.G. Jackson, "Black psychology: An avenue to the study of Afro-Americans," *Journal of Black Studies*, XII (1982), 241-260.

[2] J.A. Baldwin, "Theory and research concerning the notion of Black self-hatred: A review and reinterpretation," *Journal of Black Psychology*, V (1979), 51-77. J.A. Baldwin, R. Brown and R. Hopkins, "The Black self-hatred paradigm revisited: An Africentric analysis," in *Black Psychology*, ed. by R.L. Jones, 3rd edition (New York: Harper & Row, 1987).

26

Black personality assessment is that they all derived from the philosophical-conceptual framework of Western Psychology (i.e., European/Euro-American Psychology), and were therefore "Eurocentric" in their conceptual thrust.[3] It is not surprising then that these Eurocentric approaches to the assessment of Black personality have generated such insidious and often nefarious constructs as; low self-esteem, skin color conflicts-jealouses, self-rejection, White envy, low sense of personal causation, inability to delay gratification, learned helplessness, Black self-hatred, etc., all representing basic characterizations of the Black personality as a deficit/pathological phenomenon. These reactive and negative energy based pathogenic models of the Black personality therefore constitute a major characteristic of the Non-Africentric or Eurocentric approaches to Black personality assessment.[4]

As noted earlier, African Psychology has provided the framework for redefining and reconceptualizing the phenomenon of Black personality and its assessment. African Psychology is defined as "a system of knowledge (philosophy, definitions, concepts, models, procedures and practice) concerning the nature of the social universe from the perspective of African cosmology" or the African worldview.[5] The conceptualization (or reconceptualization) of the Black personality from the framework of African Psychology is thus based on the African worldview. The African worldview, or African cosmology, represents the basic philosophy of life of African people, encompassing African descendents dispersed throughout the world. It expresses the ethos of African people. Hence, the African worldview comprises the fundamental assumptions, beliefs and attitudes toward life, toward all of nature, and toward the universe itself that characterize African people, and thus constitutes the philosophical-ideological basis of African culture.[6] Of course, it is now becoming widely accepted that the African worldview is as old as are African people and African high cultures dating back to the Nile Valley civilizations of ancient Africa.[7]

The African worldview is governed by the overriding ontological principle of "Human-Nature unity" or "Harmony with Nature." This means that humanity forms an integral-inseparable part of nature, a "Oneness with

---

[3]Baldwin, 1976, 1979, *op. cit.*

[4]Baldwin, Brown and Hopkins, *op. cit.*

[5]*Baldwin, 1986, op. cit.*, p. 243.

[6]*Ibid*, W.W. Nobles, "African philosophy: Foundations for Black psychology," in *Black Psychology*, ed. by R.L. Jones, 2nd edition (New York: Harper & Row, 1980).

[7]Y. benJochannon, *Africa: Mother of Western Civilization* (New York: Alkebulan, 1971). Y. benJochannon, *Black Man of the Nile and his Family* (New York: Alkebulan, 1978). C.A. Diop, *The Cultural Unity of Black Africa* (Chicago: Third World Press, 1978).

Nature." All aspects of nature then are interrelated and interdependent, forming one phenomenal reality — a communal phenomenology. The African worldview is thus projected through a basic **communal phenomenology** which emphasizes oneness of being, survival of the group, commonality, interdependence, cooperation, collective responsibility and a general relational and corporate consciousness.[8] Out of this framework derives the Africentric approach to Black personality, which is, in this author's view, the only indigenous approach to the study of this phenomenon.

THE AFRICENTRIC APPROACH TO BLACK PERSONALITY

The concept of Black personality, within the Africentric framework, has been used in a variety of ways in the social science literature.[9] Chief among these notions have been the following:

a. The basic characterization of Black people's "natural" psychological functioning and behavior.

b. A system for organizing the fundamental traits of Black people's psychological functioning and behavior.

c. The cultural reality of African people manifesting itself in their basic psychological dispositions and behavior.

d. The system of psychological (spiritual, cognitive and emotional) and behavioral traits that are fundamental to Black people.

e. The sum total of all behaviors (including cognitive-emotional functioning) and other variables which enable Black people to function and interact affirmatively with their environment.

What all of these conceptualizations seem to have in common, of course, is their emphases on the concept of Black personality as representing a phenomenon which is more or less central, basic and fundamental ("natural" or culturally-based) to African/African-American people's psychological functioning and behavior (or some aspects of them). Thus, the Africentric approach to Black personality, unlike the Non-Africentric approach, is guided by a positive energy assumption where the motivational thrust of the Black personality is concerned. The motivational energy in the Black personality, according to this approach, is culturally affirmative (self-affirming) or Africentric, and is therefore "proactive' in nature, as opposed to being strictly oppression-centered/driven, and thus "reactive."

---

[8]Baldwin, 1986, *op. cit.*

[9]Baldwin, 1976, *op cit.* J.A. Baldwin, "An Africentric model of Black personality," in *Proceedings of the Thirteenth Annual Convention of ABPsi* (Washington, D.C.: ABPsi, 1980), 23-25. J.A. Baldwin, "Notes on an Africentric theory of Black personality," *The Western Journal of Black Studies*, V (1981), 172-179. Nobles, 1976, *op. cit.* R.L. Williams, *the Collective Black Mind: An Afrocentric Theory of Black Personality* (St. Louis: Williams and Associates, 1981).

A theoretical model of the Black personality developed by the author[10] and based on the Africentric paradigm will serve as the framework for this perspective on Black personality assessment. Succinctly, Baldwin's Africentric theory of Black personality asserts a basic core system of the Black personality consisting of an innate-biogenetic core called the African self-extension orientation, a partially experientially derived core called African self-consciousness, and a number of basic traits emenating from the core. The **African self-extension orientation** is the foundation of the Black personality system. It is the organizing principle of the personality system: It is an unconscious process operationally defined by the concept of spirituality. Spirituality is a dynamic interconnecting and physically transcending energy which allows the Self to merge into the totality of communal phenomenal experience: it is a "Oneness of Being" phenomenon, a communal phenomenology extending way back into the ancient reaches of the African ancestral past, as well as far into the infinite reaches of the African future.

African self-consciousness derives from the African self-extension orientation, and represents the conscious level dimension of the Black personality system. Being derived from the African self-extension orientation, African self-consciousness is partly biogenetically determined, and by nature of it being conscious, it is also partly experientially-environmentally determined. It functions as the directional aspect of the Black personality and **is undifferentiated from the African self-extension orientation under normal conditions**. African self-consciousness follows a developmental pattern. Thus, when this core system is nurtured developmentally through indigenous personal and institutional support systems, it achieves vigorous and full expression in terms of a congruent pattern of basic Africentric traits (i.e., beliefs, attitudes and behaviors which affirm African/African-American life and the authenticity of its cultural heritage).

Chief among the critical indices of the African self-consciousness construct are such attitudes and behaviors as the following:

    a. Awareness of one's African identity (a sense of collective consciousness) and African cultural heritage, and sees value in the pursuit of knowledge of Self.

    b. Recognition of African survival and proactive development as one's first priority value.

    c. Respect for and active perpetuation of all things African; African Life and African institutions.

---

[10]Baldwin, *ibid*. J.A. Baldwin, "African self-consciousness and the mental health of African-Americans," *Journal of Black Studies*, XV (1984), 177-194.

d.   A standard of conduct toward all things "non-African," and toward those things, peoples, etc., that are "anti-African."

According to Baldwin's theory, deviations from this pattern of normal functioning in the African self-consciousness core of the personality are explained in terms of variations in the personal and institutional support systems characterizing the developmental and experiential life space of the individual. Both individual differences and collective behavior among African Americans can be explained from this Africentric framework. We can see then that African self-consciousness is a key dimension of the Black personality in Baldwin's theory. It directs as well as reflects the conscious level **African survival thrust** in Black people's normal-healthy functioning. It is also that aspect of the Black personality system which has good heuristic value and can thus be assessed and studied through empirical examination. Hence, research on African self-consciousness and the predictions generated from this construct will provide for an empirical analysis of the Black personality.

AFRICENTRIC ASSESSMENT OF THE BLACK PERSONALITY: ISSUES AND FINDINGS

The significance of Africentric assessment instruments is that they are designed, more or less, within the general conceptual framework of the Africentric paradigm in Black personality theory. As previously noted, this paradigm assumes that Black behavior is culturally based, deriving from and reflecting the distinct African/African-American social reality. Thus, the African worldview comprises its own values, norms and standards undergirding Black people's behaviors. The African worldview therefore projects a **normalcy referent** for Black behavior that is independent of Euro-American culture and Western racism. Within this framework, Black behavior is conceptualized as being in the service of the authentic needs and social priorities of the African/African-American community, i.e., toward its affirmation, enhancement, survival, positive development and fulfillment of its potential as a community. Again, this normal Black behavior is neither negatively energized, nor is it merely reactive to negative and adverse environments. As previously noted, normal Black behavior, to the contrary, is positively energized (under natural conditions) and proactive in its motivational thrust. Africentric assessment instruments, then, by their very nature are sensitive to this "normal thrust" in the Black personality system as it influences African/African-American behavior.

The Africentric paradigm thus argues very effectively that given the obvious centrality of the operation of the Black personality core in the behaviors of Black people, then virtually all functionally significant behavioral patterns in this area would be expected to be influenced by this dynamic core, either in whole or in part. Heuristically speaking, this view suggests that the Black personality core, or some aspect of it, would be expected to function as either an independent variable or a moderator variable in all analyses of functionally important Black behaviors and psychological functioning. In short, assessment of the Black personality core is therefore essential to a substantive and thorough assessment and understanding of African-American behavior and functioning. In the initial response to this requirement, several major issues or concerns must be addressed in Africentric psychological research. Among these concerns are: (a) the development of cultually appropriate assessment instrumentation; (b) empirical validation of the operation of the Black personality core in African-American behavior and psychological functioning; (c) empirical assessment of the affects of cultural oppression on the Black personality.

AFRICENTRIC ASSESSMENT INSTRUMENTS

The development of Africentric assessment instrumentation has been spearheaded by a small group of researchers working independently over the past 10-15 years.[11] The earliest and bulk of activity in this general area was conducted by Robert L. Williams during the early 1970's.[12] Through his research, Dr. Williams developed some of the first Africentrically sensitive psychological measures. His repertoire of Africentric measures consist of the following:

a. **The Black Personality Questionnaire:** This is a 50-item measure surveying African-American beliefs, attitudes, behavioral and lifestyle patterns which are organized into six (6) major bipolar response sets of Black consciousness (i.e., positive or negative response sets). These response sets consist of: (1) A Pro-Black - Pro-White response set; (2) a Pan-African - NonPan-African response set; (3) a Third World — NonThird World response set; (4) an Anti-White - NonAnti-White response set; (5) A NonAnti-Black - Anti-Black response set; (6) a NonPro-White - NonPro-Black response set. An example of an item from this measure is: "When Black people move into a

---

[11]Baldwin, 1976, *op. cit.* J.A. Baldwin and Y.R. Bell, "The African self-consciousness scale An Africentric personality questionnaire," *The Western Journal of Black Studies,* IX (1985), 61-68. W.W. Nobles, "Toward an empirical and theoretical framework for defining Black families," *Journal of Marriage and Family,* XXXX (9178), 679-687. W.W. Nobles and L. Goddard, *Understanding the Black Family* (Oakland, CA: Institute for Advanced Study of Black Family Life and Culture, 1986). Williams, *op. cit.* B.J. Wright and V.R. Isenstein, *Psychological Tests and Minorities* (DHEW, Publication No. ADM. 78-482, Washington, D.C.: Government Printing Office, 1977).

[12]Williams, *op. cit.* Wright and Isenstein, *idid.*

community it tends to become run down." Items are scored in terms of "agree" or "disagree" responses.

b. **The Black Preference Inventory:** This is a 22-item measure of various life preferences of African-Americans, such as personal, social, cultural, educational and political preferences. Most of the items occur in a multiple choice format while some items require mere yes or no responses. An example of an item from this measure is: "Where do you prefer to live?" The response options are: (a) all-Black community (b) a racially mixed community (c) does not matter. Subjects are also allowed to make comments following each item. Pro-Black and anti-Black preferences are scored directly.

c. **The Black Opinion Scale:** This measure consists of an alphabetical list of ten (10) values which the subject is asked to rank from least important to most important for Black people. The values include such concepts as unity, power, etc., and the subject is instructed to rank the list from 1 to 10, with 10 representing the lowest rank and 1 the highest.

d. **The Themes of Black Awareness Test:** This is a 40-item sentence completion test which attempts to elicit thematic material related to the subject's level of Black awareness. A sentence stem is presented and the subject is asked to complete the sentence. An example of these items are: "The Black woman _____ ," or "Most Black people _____ ." Different scoring schemes can be developed depending on the kind of information sought.

e. **The Themes Concerning Blacks Test:** This measure consists of 20 charcoal drawings of a variety of possible African-American life situations. Subjects are asked to tell what they see in the pictures, what happened just before the scene in the picture, and what is going to happen next. All 20 pictures or only some of them can be used depending on the kind of information sought. Different scoring schemes can also be developed for this measure, again, depending on the information desired.

Of these five instruments, only the Black Personality Questionnaire has enjoyed limited research use outside of Williams' preliminary work.[13] Other data collected by Williams and his Associates using all of the measures are still being analyzed.[14] Thus, the full extent of the usefulness of these various

---

[13]D.A. Azibo, "Some psychological concomitants and consequences of the Black personality: Mental health implications," *Journal of Non-White Concerns* (January 1983a), 59-66. Wright and Isenstein, *ibid.*

[14]Williams, *op. cit.* Wright and isenstein, *ibid.*

measures as Black personality assessment instruments remains to be determined by future research.

The author and his Associates[15] have also developed a relevant research program in the area of Black personality assessment based on the Africentric paradigm. It is argued here that Africentric personality assessment can be most effectively conducted when the assessment instruments are firmly grounded in explicit Africentric theory, i.e., the instrument should derive directly from the construct or an explicit theoretical framework. Hence, the Black personality assessment instrument used in this research program derives from Baldwin's Africentric theory of Black personality discussed earlier, where the construct of African self-consciousness — as was noted — is a central component. The instrument is therefore appropriately called the **African Self-Consciousness (ASC) Scale.**[16] A brief description of this scale follows:

The ASC Scale is a 42-item questionnaire designed to assess African self-consciousness. The items are organized into four competency dimensions of African self-consciousness and six manifest dimensions of African self-consciousness. The four competencies are: (1) awareness/recognition of one's African identity and heritage; (2) general ideological and activity priorities placed on Black survival, liberation and proactive/affirmative development; (3) specific activity priorities placed on self-knowledge and self-affirmation, i.e., Africentric values, customs, institutions, etc.; (4) a posture of resolute resistance toward anti-Black forces, and threats to Black survival in general. The six manifest dimensions cover the areas of education, family, religion, cultural activities, interpersonal relations, and political orientation. Items alternate from negative to positive skewing toward African self-consciousness and responses occur on an eight-point scale from strongly disagree to strongly agree. An example of a negative item is: "I feel little sense of commitment to Black people who are not close friends or relatives." An example of a positive item is: "The success of an individual Black person is not as important as the survival of all Black people."

BLACK PERSONALITY TESTING AND RESEARCH SUPPORT FOR AFRICENTRIC BLACK PERSONALITY THEORY

Recent Africentric research in this pioneering area of study have begun to generate empirical support for Black personality theory utilizing these kinds of assessment instruments. Most findings in this area suggest a strong

---

[15]Baldwin and Bell, *op. cit.* J.A. Baldwin, J.A. Duncan and Y.R. Bell, "Assessment of African self-consciousness among Black students from two college environments." *Journal of Black Psychology* (1987) Vol. 13, #2.

[16]Baldwin and Bell, *ibid.*

correlation between high levels of African self-consciousness (variously conceptualized) and positive or efficacious psychological functioning and behavior among Black people.[17]

One example of these recent findings occurs in a study by Alpha Curry.[18] Curry used two measures to assess African self-consciousness: (a) The African Cultural Ideology Scale (ACIS), designed to assess dimensions of the African worldview, and (b) The Subjective Values Inventory (SVI), a measure that elicits information about descriptive differences and similarities in the meaning of concepts. She administered these measures to 100 African-Americans and 53 African-born Blacks who were students at the same university. The ACIS results were subjected to factors analysis which produced seven factors for both groups. Factors emerging for the African-Americans included: (1) pride in African heritage; (2) pride in personal qualities; (3) communalism; (4) preference for Black solidarity; (5) disillusionment with intercontinental Black solidarity; (6) dissatisfaction with integration; (7) moderate Black solidarity and communalism. The factors emerging for the combined groups included: (1) ambivalence between individuality and solidarity; (2) solidarity and group identification; (3) preserved individuality with an African identification; (4) ambivalent integrationist; (5) acceptance of African ideals; (6) socialist African self-assertiveness; (7) personal preference for autonomy. The results of the SVI indicated that African-Americans and African-born Blacks perceive their relationship to their environment in terms of cooperative and interdependent social relations. These results were generally supported by the ACIS results. Curry concluded that her findings supported the belief that African-Americans and African-born Blacks are far too similar to one another to ignore the interdependent interactions that exist between African descendants throughout the world.

A couple of studies by Azibo generated significant positive correlations between African self-consciousness and personal causation, and pro-Black preferences.[19] In one study, using content analysis of subjects' story protocols as a measure of personal causation (i.e., intrinsic-communal motivation) and Williams' Black Personality Questionnaire as a measure of African self-consciousness, Azibo found that African self-consciousness accounted for a substantial amount of the variance in personal causation. The African-

---

[17]Azibo, *op. cit*. Baldwin, Duncan and Bell, *op. cit*. Williams, *op. cit*.

[18]A.O. Curry, "An Afrikan worldview exploratory examination of traditional attitudes, values and personality correlates of Black Afrikan people" (unpublished Ph.D. dissertation, Pennsylvania State University, 1981).

[19]Azibo, *op. cit*. D.A. Azibo, "Perceived attractiveness and the Black personality." *The Western Journal of Black Studies*, VII (1983b), 229-238.

Americans who obtained the higher African self-consciousness scores evidenced more intrinsic-communal motivation in their story protocols than did the lower scoring subjects. In another study, Azibo found that Blacks who obtained higher scores on Williams' Black Personality Questionnaire also rated photographs of Black females as more attractive and more favorable than photographs of White females. Low scorers rated the Black and White photographs practically equivalent.

Gibson expanded upon Azibo's findings on the relationship between African self-consciousness and personal causation, where the latter was conceptualized in terms of internal-external locus of control (I-E).[20] Gibson used the ASC Scale and an Africentric measure of the I-E construct. The Africentric I-E measure defined externality in terms of **collective efficacy** and **corporate responsibility**, consistent with the communal-holistic principles of the African worldview. This measure also emphasized item content relevant to African-American everyday life experiences. She administered the ASC Scale and the Africentric I-E measure to 50 Black college students and found a significant positive correlation between ASC Scale scores and external personal causation scores. Those students who obtained higher ASC Scale scores also tended to be more externally (collective-communal) oriented in their explanations of causality and determinism in their lives than were the low ASC Scale scoring students. Gibson speculated on the basis of her findings that perhaps African self-consciousness fosters Africentric attributions.

Beyond Gibson's research, there have been only a few other studies that have specifically attempted to empirically assess African self-consciousness in relation to functionally significant African-American behaviors. Most of this work is currently in-progress by the author and his Associates at Florida A & M University.[21] In a recently completed study, the relationship between ASC Scale scoring patterns and certain background and situational characteristics were investigated. The ASC Scale and a background questionnaire were administered to 250 Black college students, half of whom were from a predominantly Black university setting and half were from a predominantly White university setting. Significant relationships were obtained between ASC Scale scores and the two settings as well as several background factors. Specifically, it was found that students from the predominantly Black setting obtained significantly higher ASC Scale scores than students from the predominantly White setting. It was also found that older/upper-classmen obtained significantly higher ASC Scale scores than did younger/underclassmen.

[20]See Baldwin, Duncan and Bell *op. cit.*
[21]*Ibid.*

Additionally, students who had taken Black studies courses scored significantly higher on the ASC Scale than students without this experience, and students from the predominantly Black setting who also had attended Black elementary schools obtained higher ASC Scale scores than did the other students. It was concluded that these findings strongly support the belief that African self-consciousness is an important factor in interpreting differences in psychological functioning and behaviors among Black college students, and that Black community settings may indeed have a positive affect on African self-consciousness development as the theory predicts.

FUTURE RESEARCH CONSIDERATIONS IN BLACK PERSONALITY ASSESSMENT

Other research utilizing the ASC Scale that is currently underway involve investigating the relationships between ASC Scale scores and certain communal/social-interactive developmental factors, such as early childhood socialization experiences in parent-child interactions, cultural indoctrination, cultural role models, etc. In addition, research is also underway investigating the relationship between ASC Scale scores and academic motivation and achievement, as well as additional studies of the internal consistency of the ASC Scale itself, and the relationship between the ASC Scale and other Africentric assessment instruments. Future studies are being planned to investigate the relationships between ASC Scale scoring patterns and a variety of social behaviors and preferences (i.e., Black male-female relationships, interracial preferences, etc.), stress tolerance and coping skills, and self-affirming expectations and behaviors.

Thus, the growing body of Black personality assessment studies using the ASC Scale and other relevant Africentric measures are beginning to generate supportive preliminary evidence for Africentric Black personality theory. The data generated to date clearly support the predicted strong influence that the Black personality core dimension of African self-consciousness exerts on African-American behavior and psychological functioning. Africentric Black personality assessment therefore seems to have tremendous potential as a viable and critically significant approach to the study of the Black personality, and toward our better understanding of and more effective intervention into the problems of African-American mental health.

Of course, more work is needed in this developing area of African Psychology. There is little question, however, that only through the development of Africentric assessment instruments and research strategies will we be able to generate a more accurate and reliable pool of knowledge of the African-American personality, and a more effective resolution of our current mental health crisis.

Standardized Tests and African-American Children: Communication and Language Issues

Orlando L. Taylor and Dorian Latham Lee

Introduction and Background

Virtually all standardized tests, irrespective of type, rely heavily on communicative behavior. Verbal language, both oral and written, is the most frequent type of communicative behavior utilized in standardized tests, sometimes as an expression function and other times as a comprehension function.[1] Even if a given standardized test does not depend on communicative behavior or verbal language as test stimuli or as a response mode, communication and verbal language are central elements in the interaction dimension that occurs between test giver and taker throughout the "moment of assessment". Moreover, communication and language, both verbal or non-verbal, are typically used to present test directions, to reinforce behavior during assessments and to encourage subject performance.

In the past two decades, it is a well documented fact that incongruencies between the communicative behavior or language of the test giver (or test constructor) and the test taker can result in test bias (c.f., Taylor and Payne, Seymour and Miller-Jones, and Vaughn-Cooke[2]). The notion that tests and other assessment procedures should not be linguistically or culturally discriminatory has been upheld by several important court decisions including Larry P. v. Riles (1972), Diana v. State Board of Education (1970), Mattie T. v. Holladay (1977) and ultimately in Public Law 94-142 and its subsequent amendments.[3]

---

[1]Throughout this paper, the term "communication" will be used to include any type of human behavior which is used to transmit information between a minimum of two persons. "Verbal language", a type of communicative behavior, will refer to the use of linguistic codes to represent meaning in communicative situations. In addition to verbal language, communication also includes the use of nonverbal communicative behaviors, rhetorical style, discourse rules, narrative style, conversational rules, etc. One's competence in using the full range of communicative behavior within a given cultural context is referred to as "communicative competence".

[2]Taylor, O. and Payne, K., *Culturally valid testing: A proactive approach.* Topics in Language Disorders 3 (1983); Seymour, H. and Miller-Jones, D., Language and Cognitive Assessment of Black Children. In N. Lass (Ed.), Speech and Language: Advances in Basic Research and Practice. (New York: Academic Press, 1981); Vaughn-Cooke, F.B., Improving language assessment in minority children, ASHA, 25 (Sept., 1983) pp. 29-34.

[3]Larry P. v. Riles, Civil Action No. 0-71-2270, 343 F. Supp. 1306 (N.D. Cal., 1972); Dianna v. State Board of Education, C.A. 70 RFT (N.D. Cal., Feb. 3, 1970); Mattie T. v. Holladay, 552f. Supp. 72 (N.D. Miss., 1977); Public Law 94-142, The Education of All Handicapped Children Act (Nov. 29. 1975).

Specifically, Public Law 94-142 states that:

a) testing and evaluation materials and procedures must be selected and administered so that they are not racially or culturally discriminatory.

b) testing and evaluation materials must be provided and administered in the language or other mode of communication in which the child is most proficient.

c) tests must be administered to a child with a motor, speech, hearing, visual or other communication disability, or to a bilingual child, so as to reflect accurately the child's ability in the area tested, rather than the child's impaired communication skill or limited English language skill.

Despite the requirements of federal law and the aforementioned court decisions, few standardized tests take culturally based communication or language issues into account at any level of the assessment process. Indeed, most standardized tests, and the communicative environments in which they are administered are culturally discriminatory against many cultural groups in the United States, since specific norms have not been established for them, and since insufficient numbers of persons from the groups are typically included in norming samples. African-Americans, the nation's largest "minority group" are among the groups most vulnerable to test bias, particularly those persons who come from low income, poorly educated or socially isolated communities. Finally, tests of specific language function, as well as those which use language to assess other cognitive, social or psychological functions, often measure knowledge of Standard English, rather than human development, aptitude or achievement in the presumed area under assessment.

The purpose of this paper will be to: a) summarize the available data on sources of communication bias in standardized tests with specific reference to African-Americans, and b) present some suggestions for resolving such bias.

Sources of Culturally-Based Communication and Language Bias in Standardized Tests

There are several possible sources of culturally-based communication and language bias in standardized tests. Five major types of such bias are:

a) situational bias
b) linguistic bias
c) communicative style bias
d) cognitive style bias
e) interpretation bias

Situational Bias

Taylor and Payne have presented rather persuasive evidence to show that the social interactive dimension between test taker and test giver can be a major source of bias in the testing process. Using contemporary pragmatic theory as the bases for their arguments, Taylor and Payne claim that one might view all assessments including the administration of standardized tests as social occasions, with expected communicative rules by both the test giver and the test taker. Furthermore, they claim that the eliciting, recording, and/or evaluating of behaviors produced by a test taker is done, by necessity, within the framework of a set of communication rules. They posit that mismatches can occur between tester and test takers with respect to the social rules of language interaction. Some of the major areas of potential mismatch include rules of who may speak to whom, appropriate elicitation procedures, appropriate language behaviors, behaviors which may serve as a communication, and rules of production and interpretation.

Because of these interactional rules, silence — which in and of itself may be a communicative device — may be misinterpreted as a marker of deficiency or pathology when it is indeed considered appropriate by the speaker. In the special case of standardized tests in which a tester from a given cultural group seeks responses to obvious questions, the respondent may choose to give no response, or give an answer which is mistakenly perceived as one which the testor wishes to receive. In any case, the testee is likely to produce responses which are perceived as appropriate within the framework of the topic, situation and context of the test administration environment. Testor misinterpretation, misunderstanding, or rejection of the test taker's output can lead to faulty assessments of cognitive, social or language behavior.

Saville-Troike[5] has provided very graphic examples of client/assessor mismatches which can negatively impact upon the social/situational dimension of standardized testing. Kochman and Mitchell-Kernan and Kernan are among a small, but growing, group of anthropologists who have documented Black-White differences in communicative expectations and behaviors in a variety of social situations and social purposes.[6]

---

[4]Taylor and Payne, *Culturally valid testing: A proactive approach*, pp. 8-20.

[5]Saville-Troike, M., *The Ethnography of Communication*, (Baltimore: University Park Press, 1982).

[6]Kochman, T., *Black and White: Styles and Conflict*. (Chicago: University of Chicago Press, 1981); Mitchell-Kernan, C. and Kernan, K.T. *Pragmatics of Directive Choice Among Children*. In S. Ervin-Tripp and C. Mitchell-Kernan (Eds.), *Child Discourse*. (New York: Academic Press, 1977).

Linguistic Bias

The greatest and most impressive body of literature that has been written on communication and language based sources of bias in standardized tests, especially as related to African-American persons is in the area of linguistic bias. In view of the abundance of research which has emerged on communication and language behaviors of African-Americans by linguists and ethnographers, it is unsurprising that linguistic issues of test bias have dominated the literature.

There is much debate on the current nature of contemporary African-American language. On the one hand, such scholars as Labov[7] argue that these speech behaviors are diverging **more** from Standard American English than ever before because of increasing segregation between White and African-American communities. On the other side of this controversy, such scholars, as Vaughn-Cooke[8] argue that African-American speech is moving towards convergence with Standard English.

Perhaps the most proper conclusion to draw is that the African-American speech community is highly diversified, resulting in various amounts and types of incongruity between test takers from these communities and the communicative assumptions of most standardized tests. These incongruencies may emerge in any aspect of language. Wolfram, Taylor and Reveron[9] for example, have shown how speakers of what is often referred to as Black English Vernacular (BEV) might make errors in responding to test items written in Standard English when they in fact, have knowledge of the information contained in the item.

For example, in the Wepman Test of Auditory Discrimination (WTAD)[10], a test in which testees are required to make phonological distinctions between pairs of words, such as pin/pen and wreath/reef, BEV speakers (as opposed to Black Standard English speakers) may encounter difficulty because many of the presumed contrasting pairs are pronounced alike. Since this particular test requires BEV speakers to make phonemic distinctions which typically do not occur in their native dialect, the WTAD is likely to

[7]Labov, W., *The Increasing Divergence of Black and White Vernaculars: Introduction to the Research Reports* (Unpublished manuscript, 1985).

[8]Vaughn-Cooke, F.B., *Improving language assessment in minority children*, ASHA, 25 (September, 1983) pp. 29-34.

[9]Wolfram, W., Test interpretation and sociolinguistic differences. *Topics in Language* Disorders, 3 (June, 1983), pp. 21-34; Taylor, O. Language issues and testing, *Journal of Nonwhite Concerns*. (April, 1978), pp. 125-133; Reveron, W.W., *The acquisition of four Black English morphological rules by Black preschool children* (Ohio State University: Unpublished Doctoral Dissertation. 1978).

[10]Wepman, J.M. *Auditory Discrimination Test*, (Chicago: Language Research Associates, 1958).

underestimate the development of auditory perceptual skills in many young African-American children.

On the Illinois Test of Psycholinguistic Abilities (ITPA)[11], Wolfram, et. al[12] have shown that African-American children who use nonstandard forms, e.g., hisself for himself, or twenty cent for twenty cents, typically have their normal and age-appropriate indigenous language responses scored as being incorrect. In addition, their overall test performance is frequently categorized falsely as being suggestive of language or cognitive delay.

In the area of vocabulary, Roberts[13] has claimed that thirteen of the first fifty items on the Peabody Picture Vocabulary Test (PPVT) are biased against speakers of BEV, either because of unfamiliarity, different pronunciations or different meaning. Since each item on this test carries an age weighting of approximately three months, these thirteen potentially biased items could result in an error of up to thirty-nine months in the assessment of vocabulary development in many African-American children.

Problems of the above types are also seen in many psychological and educational tests, including such popular instruments as the Metropolitan Achievement Test, the Comprehensive Test of Basic Skills and the Standford Early School Achievement Test. Hoover, Politzer and Taylor[14] have provided detailed examples of linguistically based biases in these tests against African-Americans.

Communicative Style Bias

Another major assumption of most standardized tests is that all individuals communicate their experiences in a similar manner. Therefore, standardized tests tend to implicitly infer a test taker's ability from a predetermined standard for using language to impart information obtained from life experiences. Cultural differences in language use can, and often do, interfere with the validity of behavioral evidence derived from test takers.

The study of language within the social context in which it occurs (i.e., the communicative environment) has led to the identification of variances in the manner in which information is imparted among and within cultural

---

[11]Kirk, S., McCarthy, J., and Kirk, W., *Illinois Test of Psycholinguistic Abilities.* (Urbanna II: University of Illinois Press, 1968).

[12]Wolfram, W., Williams, R. and Taylor, O., Some predicted dialect interference in select language development tests. (Short course presented at the Annual Convention of the American Speech-Language and Hearing Association, Rockville, MD, 1972).

[13]Roberts, E. *An Evaluation of standardized tests as tools of measurement of language development,* Language Research Reports, No. 1, (Cambridge, Mass.: Language Research Foundation, 1970).

[14]Hoover, M., Politzer, R. and Taylor, O. Bias in achievement and diagnostic reading tests: A Linguistically Oriented View (Unpublished paper, National Conference on Test Bias, National Institute of Education, 1974).

groups. The manner of imparting information is often referred to as communicative style. Many scholars suggest that they communicative style used by an individual results from a combination of socially and culturally determined factors such as values, interactional rules and perceptions of events. Such differences of communicative style may interfere with the standardized testing process.

For example, differences in communicative style may interfere with the validity of the tester's early impressionistic observations of the testee. Test takers who use a culturally preferred communicative style of lengthy social greetings may be incorrectly viewed as exhibiting avoidance behaviors by testers who expect a style which requires rapid approaching of the main purpose of communication. Likewise, test takers who use a culturally preferred communicative style which requires the use of silence may be viewed as lacking verbal skills by testers who expect a style which promotes verbosity.

Differences in communicative style also interfere with the validity of performance observations. Standardized test protocols are typically based on eliciting a communicative style which requires verbosity and the stating of obvious information. Variations from the expected communicative style often results in a judgement of low performance or low ability.[15]

Attempts by test designers to restrict or control the communicative and interactive nature of the environment have not always been compatible with the communicative styles that individuals from various cultures bring to the testing situation. Saville-Troike[16] has presented a classic example to illustrate this point. She reports that her communicative style of direct questioning to obtain language samples from Navajo children was at variance with their style of engaging in silent interaction before verbal interaction. Thus, in order to obtain valid language samples, Saville-Troike found it necessary to adjust her communicative style during the assessments rather than force a change of style by the children. Likewise, many test administrators are often frustrated or erroneously conclude that young African-American children lack ability when they use a communicative style which prohibits responding to "obvious" questions with "obvious" answers. Ward[17] has empirically demonstrated that many working-class African-Americans use a communicative style which devalues the expression of "obvious" information.

---

[15]Wolfram, W., Williams, R. and Taylor, O., *Some predicted dialect interference*, 1972.

[16]Saville-Troike, M., *The Ethnography of Communication*, (Baltimore: University Park Press, 1982).

[17]Ward, M.C., *Them children: A study in language learning*, (New York: Holt, Rinehart and Winston, 1971).

Another protocol used by standardized tests to infer ability is story-telling. It has been reported that the communicative styles used to tell stories vary across socio-cultural groups (Heath; Michaels; Michaels and Collins).[18] Michaels[19] has delineated the features associated with two communicative styles used to tell stories (i.e., topic-centered and topic-associating). The topic-centered style is the style most often expected by standardized tests. The topic-centered is characterized by: (1) structured discourse on a single topic, (2) elaboration upon the topic and (3) lack of presupposing shared knowledge.

A second style, topic-associating, is not the expected communicative style for story-telling for most standardized tests. The topic-associating style is characterized by: (1) structured discourse on several linked topics, (2) presupposition of shared knowledge and (3) lack of consideration for detail. While this style is the preferred style of story-telling among many working-class African-Americans, it is not regarded as story-telling ability by standardized tests. The stories told by African-American children who use the topic-associating communicative style are often viewed as disorganized and/or pointless. As a result, these children are often labelled as language disordered, learning disabled or in extreme cases emotionally disturbed.[20] These examples illustrate that a lack of consideration for variance in communicative styles among and within cultural groups can result in the development of standardized tests which are invalid for many segments of the population.

Cognitive style

Standardized tests tend to also be based on the erroneous assumption that all individuals evidence ability through the use of a similar cognitive style. Cognitive style is defined as the manner in which individuals perceive, organize the process experiences. Cognitive style is viewed as a behavioral tendency which is believed to guide and shape an individual's response to an experience.[21]

As with communicative style, variance among and within groups of individuals with respect to the type of preferred cognitive style exhibited has

---

[18]Heath, S.B., What no bedtime story means: Narrative skills at home and school. *Language in Society* II, (1982): 49-76; Michaels, S. 'Sharing time': Children's narrative styles and differential access to literacy. *Language and Society*. 10 (1981): 423-442; Michaels, S. and Collins, J., Oral discourse styles: Classroom interaction and the acquisition of literacy. In D. Tannen (Ed.) *Coherence on Spoken and Writeen Discourse*. (Norwood, N.J.: Ablex, 1984).

[19]Michaels, 'Sharing Time', pp. 423-442.

[20]Feagans. L. The Language of Children Reared in Poverty: Implications for Education and Intervention, (New York: Academic Press, 1982).

[21]Messick, S. and Associates, *Individuality in Learning: Implications of Cognitive Styles and Creativity for Human Development*, (San Francisco, CA: Jossey-Bass, Inc., Publishers, 1976).

been well documented.[22] Nine different cognitive styles have been delineated, including: (1) field dependence-independence, (2) analytic-relational, or (3) impulsivity-reflectivity. (See Goldstein and Blackman[23] for a complete listing and discussion.)

A preference towards a particular cognitive style is thought to be guided by sociocultural factors. There is evidence, for example, which suggests that individuals of African and Hispanic descent tend to exhibit a higher frequency of preference towards a relational-field dependent cognitive style, whereas individuals of Asian and European descent tend to exhibit a higher preference towards an analytic-field independent cognitive style.[24]

Cognitive style differences have also been found to correlate with gender and economic factors. For example, females have been reported to exhibit a higher frequency of tendency towards field dependence when compared with males.[25] Individuals from a middle-class background have been reported to exhibit a tendency towards field independence when compared with individuals from working-class backgrounds.[26]

Correlations associated with a preference toward a particular cognitive style and variables such as ethnicity, economic levels and gender have been hypothesized to be due to child rearing practices.[27] Such differences, according to Hale simply reflect different ways of knowing and problem-solving, not differences in ability.[28]

As mentioned earlier, standardized tests are often based on the assumption that all individuals may evidence ability by using a similar cognitive

---

[22]Kagan, J. and Kogan, N., Individual variation in cognitive processes. In P. Mussen (Ed.), Carmichael's *Manual of Child Psychology*, third edition, volume one, (New York: Wiley Publishers, 1970); Kogan, N., Cognitive Styles in Infancy and Early Childhood, (Hillsdale, N.J.: Lawrence Erlbaum Associates, 1976; Witkin, H.A. and Goodenough, D.R., *Cognitive styles: Essence and origins. Field dependence and field independence*, Psychological Issues Monograph 51, (International Universities Press, 1981).

[23]Goldstein, K. and Blackman, S., *Cognitive Styles: Five Approaches and Relevant Research*, (New York: John Wiley and Sons, 1978).

[24]Ramirez, M. and Price-Williams, D. Cognitive styles of children of three ethnic groups in the United States, *Journal of Cross-Cultural Psychology*, 5 (1974), pp. 212-219.

[25]Kogan, N. *Cognitive Styles in Infancy and Early Childhood*, (Hillsdale, N.J.: Lawrence Erlbaum Associates, 1976); Witkin, H.A. *Cognitive styles in academic performance and in teacher-student relations*. In Messick (Ed.) *Individuality in Learning: Implications of cognitive style and creativity for Human Development*, (San Francisco, CA: Jossey-Bass, 1976).

[26]Ramirez, M. and Price-Williams, D., Cognitive styles of children of three ethnic groups in the United States, *Journal of Cross-Cultural Psychology*, 5 (1974), pp. 212-219.

[27]Hale, J. *Black Children: Their Roots, Culture and Learning Styles*. (Utah: Brigham Young University Press, 1982); Ramirez, M. and Castaneda, A., *Cultural Democracy, Bicognitive Development and Education*, (New York: Academic Press, 1974).

[28]Hale, *Black Children*, 1982.

style. The Wepman Test of Auditory discrimination (WTAD)[29] illustrates this point. In addition to linguistically caused sources of bias, this test is also biased towards an analytic cognitive style. The items on this standardized test require the use of an analytic cognitive style; thereby ignoring or penalizing the use of an opposing relational style (a style reported to be more often preferred by African-Americans). While the WTAD is capable of providing one indication of auditory discrimination ability, its elicitation paradigm is not the only valid indicator of this function.

For example, the WTAD does not allow an individual to express auditory discrimination skills by distinguishing between various gestalts, e.g., a task that requires discrimination of the prosodic patterns of various languages. While such a task may require a difference cognitive style (i.e., relational), it may also be a valid indicator of auditory discrimination skills for persons who do not prefer an analytic cognitive style of perceiving reality.

There are data which suggest that one's cognitive style may influence language style. These data suggest that African-American children from a working-class background have a tendency to use a style of language which may be viewed as context-dependent, while Euro-American children from a working-class background have a tendency to use context-independent language.[30]

Context-dependent language may be characterized as language whose meaning is primarily based upon the immediate context in which it occurs.[31] Children who frequently use a context-dependent language style are reported to: (1) use more ellipticals than non-ellipticals[32] (2) use more pronouns than nouns,[33] and (3) support their verbal language with nonverbal language.[34] Thus, in order to determine the "meaning" of utterances from persons preferring this cognitive style consideration of the context in which language is produced is essential. In other words, since the context-dependent language style is highly flexible, variable and adaptable, "meaning" changes as the context changes.

Conversely, context-independent language may be characterized as language whose meaning is explicit and may be determined independent of the

---

[29]Wepman, *Test of Auditory Discrimination*, 1958.

[30]Hilliard, Alternatives to IQ Testing, 1976.

[31]Ibid., 1976.

[32]Cohan, Conceptual styles, 1969.

[33]Bloom, L. One Word At A Time: The Use of Single Word Utterances Before Syntax, (The Hague:Mouton, 1973); nelson, K., Individual differences in language: Implications for development and language, *Developmental Psychology*, 17 1981), pp. 170-187.

[34]Dore, J., A pragmatic description of early language development, *Journal of Psycholinguistic Research*, 4 (1974), pp. 343-350.

context in which is occurs.[35] Children who frequently use a context-independent language style are reported to: (1) use more non-ellipticals than ellipticals,[36] (2) use more nouns than pronouns,[37] and (3) to rarely use nonverbal language to enhance language meaning.[38] It may be argued that the context-independent language style is rigid, controlled and predictable. Meanings of utterances are exact.

Standardized tests which fail to recognize differences in language style fail to accurately determine ability. The Verbal Expression subtest of the Illinois Test of Psycholinguistic Abilities (ITPA)[39] can be cited as an example of a standardized test which fails to consider differences in cognitive style. This subtest presents individual objects to a child and asks him/her to express all s/he can about the object. For those children guided by the context-dependent language style, there is little information for them to make interpretative expressions because the object is not within a social, functional or communicative context. The Verbal Expression subtest of the ITPA also penalizes the child if s/he chooses to use gestures to support his/her verbal language. In other words, this subtest is based on the assumption that an explicit verbal language style is the only means of presenting information and penalizes the use of other styles.

Test Interpretation Bias

A tester's interpretation of a test taker's ability is derived from comparisons of his/her behavioral responses to a task in relation to the behavioral responses on the same task by a norming sample. The concept of a universal norm has been challenged by many scholars on the grounds that not all children develop the same skills at the same developmental age or in the same developmental sequence. For example, child language research demonstrates that some children develop the use of pronouns before the development of an extensive noun vocabulary. For others, the reverse pattern of development occurs.[40] Thus, standardized tests which expect extensive noun development at a certain chronological age will falsely identify children with a different language development profile as being language delayed or disordered.

---

[35]Hilliard, Alternatives to IQ Testing, 1976.

[36]Cohan, Conceptual styles, 1969.

[37]Bloom, One Word At A Time, 1973; Nelson, Individual differences in language, 1981.

[38]Dore, A pragmatic description, 1974.

[39]Kirk, McCarthy and Kirk, ITPA, 1968.

[40]Williams, R. and Wolfram, W. *Social Dialects: Differences versus disorders*, (Rockville, MD: American Speech and Hearing Association, 1977); Wolfram, W. and Fasold, R., *The Study of Social Dialects in American English*, (Englewood Cliffs, N.J.: Prentice-Hall, 1974).

Moreover, all children have not been exposed to the same variety of English during their language development period. For these reasons, standardized tests which expect universal development of phonological, morphological and syntactical rules will erroneously identify many African-American children, who develop linguistic rules which are at variance with Standard English expectations, as language delayed or disordered.

Since normative linguistic data on all varieties of English are presently unavailable, interpretations of language ability based on a normative perspective will continue to be invalid until such data exist.[41] However, the gathering of such data will not validate the assumption of a universal norm for all children within a given cultural group since all persons within a cultural group are not the same. For example, all African-Americans do not demonstrate all features of BEV in their speech. Conversely, all Whites do not evidence all features of Standard English in their speech. For these reasons, interpretations based on comparisons with group norms have their limitations. The primary limitation is the assumption that variations within a group or between groups represents a liability.

Use of Communicative and Language Data to Modify Existing Tests

While most test purists would reject the notion of modifying standardized tests, the fact still remains that these instruments can more validly assess cognitive, social and language behaviors of African-Americans if communicative and language data are used to make them more culturally sensitive. Taylor and Payne have argued that the most powerful procedure that can be employed to modify standardized tests is to conduct what one might call a sociolinguistically-based item analysis.[42]

This procedure requires the test administrator to first determine the mean mental-age (MA) or chronological-age (CA) value of each test item. Next, the test administrator analyzes the sociolinguistic and communicative assumptions of each item to determine which are likely to be biased against the speech community from which the test taker is a member. In this process, care must be taken to use the proper sub-set of the test taker's speech community (e.g., the proper gender of SES sub-group) to avoid overgeneralizations and stereotypes. Finally, the product of the number of culturally incongruent items times the mean MA/CA value per item will equal the total potential bias against persons from the test taker's speech community.

For example, if the average CA/MA value for items is three months, and eight items appear to be sociolinguistically incongruent, the total potential

---

[41]Vaughn-Cooke, *Improving Language Assessment*, 1983.
[42]Taylor and Payne, *Culturally valid testing*. 1983.

bias value of the test would be two years. With this information in hand, the examiner would then have several choices. First, s/he could add the value of potential test bias to the test taker's total score. Second, s/he could state that the test taker's total score is no less than the obtained score and no greater than the obtained score plus the value computed for total potential bias. Third, the examiner could do an item analyses to determine exactly how many of the potentially biased items were actually failed to compute a modified test bias value to add to the obtained score.

Taylor and Payne[43] have also suggested three other possible techniques which might be employed to modify existing standardized tests to make them more valid for use with African-American children. They include:

a) Change the stimuli into a parallel form that is likely to be appropriate for the cultural or linguistic group;

b) change the scoring to permit dialect alternatives to be considered correct;

c) Establish new test norms for the targeted population by obtaining typical response profiles and scores from random samples of normal persons of various age groups in the target population.

Use of Data to Construct New Tests

Standardized tests have been developed which attempt to make use of currently available linguistic data with respect to language and cultural variations. Some of these include (1) The Denver Articulation Screening Examination, (2) Test of Proficiency in Black Standard and Nonstandard English, and (3) the Screening Kit of Language Development).[44] Each of these tests attempts to consider that cultural and linguistic variability exists. These tests have modified the expected response, but appear to be based on the same flawed assumption that variation from an expected norm indicates disability. This is the same assumption which invalidates other standardized tests. Thus, individuals taking any one of these tests are at a similar risk for being penalized for exhibiting behavioral variation.

Data which challenges the assumption of universality of behavioral tendencies among individuals, which appears to underlie most standardized tests, has yet to be incorporated into standardized tests. Those tests which utilize a bidialectal referent appear to address the issue of behavioral

---

[43]Ibid.

[44]Drumwright, A., Van Natta, P., Camp, B., Frankenburg, W. and Drexler, H., The Denver Articulation Screening Exam, Journal of Speech and Hearing disorders, 38 (1973), pp. 3-14; Politzer, R., Hoover, M. and Brown, D., A test of proficiency in Black standard and nonstandard speech, TESOL Quarterly, 8 (1974), pp. 27-25; The Screening Kit of Language Development, (Baltimore: University Park Press, 1983).

variability among individuals somewhat by allowing for at least two ways of responding to a task.[45] The need for more tests which will allow for variability of response types appears evident.

Alternative Approaches to Standardized Tests

There may not be, as of yet, enough available data which would allow for the development of standardized tests which validly account for linguistic and cultural differences. This would entail the allowance of a wide variety of response types and a wide variety of tasks to elicit a single response. The nature of standardized tests, however, may preclude the development of such a test. The very purposes for which standardized tests are designed, i.e., (1) to control the environment, (2) to elicit a set of expected responses and (3) to distinguish groups using numerical ratings, preclude the incorporation of allowance for variability.

Perhaps a more practical use of contemporary linguistic data is for the development of appropriate assessment procedures other than standardized tests. Such procedures would attempt to discover strengths and weaknesses in light of various linguistic and cognitive styles. Project Spectrum, A Harvard-Tufts University project is currently in the process of gathering data for the development of this type of intelligence/achievement assessment protocol. The psychologists involved in this project are attempting to discover the various ways in which children may exhibit ability.[46] The project, at present is limited, with respect to its target population. For the most part, the subjects are children attending a University school, which may limit the amount of linguistic and cultural variation observed. At any rate, this project appears to be in the forefront of discovering new alternatives for valid testing.

Naturalistic observations and criterion referenced testing which utilize the test taker's indigenous communication and linguistic norms have been recommended by several scholars[47] (c.f. Seymour and Miller-Jones; Leonard and Weiss) The advantage of naturalistic observations and analyses of spontaneous language versus restricted elicitation paradigms is that one is freed of linguistic presuppositions, and is able to observe code-switching behaviors as a function of various situations, topics, audiences and contests. Criterion-referenced procedures, of course, permit the test administrator to

---

[45]Seymour and Miller-Jones, Language and Cognitive Assessment, 1983.

[46]Goleman, D., Rethinking the value of intelligence tests, The New York times, (Section 12, November 9, 1986).

[47]Seymour and Miller-Jones, Language and Cognitive Assessment, 1981; Leonard, L.B., and Weiss, A.L., Application of nonstandardized assessment procedures to diverse linguistic populations, Topics in Language Disorders, 3, (June, 1983), pp. 35-45.

establish a community based reference point for assessing the level of linguistic and cognitive development of African-Americans.

Finally, Vaughn-Cooke[48] has recommended several additional alternative considerations to be made in validly assessing of African-American persons:

1. Standardize existing tests on non-mainstream English speakers
2. Include a small percentage of minorities in the standardization sample when developing tests
3. Refrain from using all standardized tests that have not been corrected for test bias when assessing non-mainstream English speakers
4. Develop a new test which can provide a more appropriate assessment of non-mainstream English speakers.

Summary

On most standardized tests, African-American persons are faced with a two-fold challenge: a) performing required tasks and b) demonstrating abilities on these tasks by manipulating communicative and language codes which are frequently different from their indigenous systems. Because of these language and communicative incongruencies, African-Americans are frequently invalidly assessed. Either they fail to demonstrate the desired cognitive, social or linguistic behaviors because of flawed expectations or misinterpretations, or they fail to demonstrate the desired behaviors within the communication and language frameworks demanded by the tests.

The communication and language patterns of African-Americans, particularly those from working-class backgrounds, are frequently at variance with those expected by standardized tests. At times, these incongruencies diminish performance on standardized tests to the extent that the results fail to accurately represent actual abilities.

The body of literature on communication and language behaviors of African-American persons is growing rapidly. These data may be incorporated into the development of new standardized tests which more validly assess the abilities of the African-Americans. The data suggest, however, that the very assumptions and paradigms upon which most standardized tests are based need to be revised. Such revisions may take the form of new elicitation procedures, methods of evaluation and, most importantly, the types of behaviors chosen as being representative of certain competencies.

---

[48]Vaughn-Cooke, Improving language assessment, 1983.

Bias In Reading Tests
For Black Language Speakers:
A Sociolinguistic Perspective

by
Mary Rhodes Hoover, Robert L. Politzer and Orlando Taylor

Sociolinguists have been aware for some time that the measurement of linguistic abilities may involve strong biases because the language of examinees may differ from the one they are presumed to have by the examiner. Many scholars[1] [2] [3] [4] question the degree to which tests in standard English can measure the verbal ability of nonstandard speakers. Cazden[5] called for the creation of "dialect-fair" measures of language development some time ago.

Culturally determined differences within a language can occur at the levels of phonology, syntax, vocabulary, or referential context. The variables that consistently and predictably account for these differences include social status, age, sex, and ethnicity and their possible interactions.[6] These biases may indeed converge or interact in subtle ways and reinforce each other.

Biases are usually most apparent and most easily documentable when specific linguistic features themselves, rather than messages conveyed by language, are the chief object of the test or the test item. In other words, in tests which examine specific components of language and language skills (e.g. auditory discrimination, articulation, vocabulary) the bias will generally be revealed by a contrastive study of the speech variety of the testee and one that is desired by the examiner.[7]

[1]Dell Hymes, "Language in Education: Forward to Fundamentals,"*Language in Education: Ethnographic Essays*, Washington, D.C.: Center for Applied Linguistics, 1980.

[2]William Labov, "The Logic of Nonstandard English," G. Alatis (ed), Monograph Series in Languages and Linguistics, *20th Annual Round Table*, Washington, D.C.: Georgetown University Press, 1969.

[3]Anna Fay Vaughn-Cooke, "Improving Language Assessment in Minority Children," *ASHA*, Vol. 25, Summer 1983, pp. 25-29.

[4]Walt Wolfram, "Levels of Sociolinguistic Bias in Testing," *Black English: A Seminar*, Deborah Sears Harrison and Tom Trabasso (ed.), Lawrence Erlbaum Associates, Hillsdale, NJ: 1976.

[5]Courtney Cazden, "Subcultural Differences in Child Language: An Interdisciplinary Review," *Merrill-Palmer Quarterly of Behavior and Development*, Vol. 12, 1966, p. 204.

[6]Walt Wolfram and Ralph W. Fasold, *The Study of Social Dialects in American English*, Englewood Cliffs, NJ: Prentice Hall, Inc., 1974.

[7]P. Griffin, W. Wolfram, and D. Taylor, "A Sociolinguistic Analysis of the Armed Services Vocational Aptitude Battery," Arlington, VA: Center for Applied Linguistics, 1974.

So far, the study of linguistically caused bias has, therefore, focused chiefly on diagnostic tests of general language ability rather than on reading tests per se. To give some examples, Wolfram[8] points out that there is bias in the widely used Templin Darling Test of Articulation: Only the standard English articulation of such sounds as "th," final "r," or the "st" cluster are accepted as correct. Politzer[9], in addition to Karger[10] and Wolfram[11], has pointed out that the Wepman Test of Auditory Discrimination, in which pupils are asked to discriminate between minimal pairs (e.g. pen/pin, lave/lathe), requires the examinee to make phonemic distinctions which may have no phonemic relevance in nonstandard dialects. In the Illinois Test of Psycholinguistic Abilities (ITPA), grammatically nonstandard forms like "hisself" (for himself) or "two bed" (for two beds), which are perfectly regular within many nonstandard speakers' grammars, are simply scored wrong by the ITPA.[12] [13] Hicks[14] found similar bias in the ITPA and discovered that a test which corrected for vernacular Black English (VBE) background and Black culture gave more accurate results. Roberts[15] found that at least 13 of the first 50 items on the widely used Peabody Picture test are potentially culture specific to speakers of standard English only.

The IQ test, also a type of language test in its verbal items, is often culturally and economically biased.[16] A typical example is as follows: Children are shown a picture of a man dressed in a suit and carrying a brief case. They are asked "Where is the man going?" The correct answer is "to work." Working class children, whose fathers may wear a suit only on formal occasions, will invariably answer "to church," thereby lowering their

[8]Wolfram, "Levels of..."

[9]Robert Politzer, "Reading Discrimination and the Disadvantaged," *The English Record*, Vol. 21, 1971, pp. 174-179.

[10]G. Karger, "The Performance of Lower Class Black and Lower Class White Chuildren on the Wepman Auditory Discrimination Test: The Effects of Dialect and Training and the Relationship to Reading Achievement," Ed.D. dissertation, Harvard University, 1973.

[11]Wolfram, "Levels of..."

[12]Walter Wolfram and Donna Christian, "On Application of Sociolinguistic Information: Test Evaluation and Dialect Differences in Appalachia," *Standards and Dialects in English*, ed. J.M. Williams, Cambridge, MA: Winthrop, 1980.

[13]Wolfram and Fasold, *The Study of...*

[14]Shirley F. Hicks, "The Assessment of Certain Linguistic-Cognitive Skills in the Low Income Black Child Revisited," Stanford, CA: Stanford University School of Education, Ph.D. Thesis, 1979.

[15]E. Roberts, "An Evaluation of Standardized Tests as Tools of Measurement of Language Development," *Language Research Reports*, No. 1, Cambridge, MA: Language Research Laboratory, 1970.

[16]Jim Cummins, *Bilingualism and Special Education: Issues in Assessment and Pedagogy*, Clevedon, Avon, England: Multilingual Matters, Ltd., 1984.

IQ by many critical points. Williams[17] found that for Blacks dominant in VBE rather than in standard English, a VBE version of an IQ test raised IQ scores significantly. The use of pictures showing Blacks and related to Black culture raised IQ scores for all Black children.

This article is, of course, primarily concerned with reading tests, not the diagnostic language ability tests referred to above. Yet language ability tests like the Wepman test or the ITPA are often used as diagnostic instruments, especially at the kindergarten level. Interpretations of language ability based on these tests may very well give rise to self-fulfilling hypotheses concerning the probable reading failure of children who are not dominant in standard English. Moreover, the specific testing of isolated language skills so characteristic of these instruments is also built into several of the most widely used tests of reading achievement.

Another limitation of this inquiry is that our analysis focuses primarily on bias detectable in the tests themselves and not on cultural and linguistic biases which may be involved in the testing situation. Linguistic and cultural differences between the pupil's performance and the examiner's expectation can be involved in the very activity called testing and can, by themselves, have considerable impact on the outcome of a test. These influences can be examined from a sociolinguistic or sociological point of view, for instance, by ethnomethodologically oriented sociologists (e.g., Cicourel et al.[18]).

An example of differences in perception of the testing situation is seen in the assumption of standardized test authors that is perfectly appropriate for the testee to (1) be willing to provide obvious information (e.g., how many eyes do you have) and (2) give a performance for a total stranger (the examiner). These basic social assumptions may be in direct conflict with interactional rules for children in some cultures. That is, some children may fail to respond to items on a test for reasons that are not related to the items themselves, but to the task expected of them. We hypothesize that children from working class populations — especially Black — are less oriented to public performance of the obvious to unfamiliar adults than are middle class children — particularly Whites. The latter, we believe, tend to be programmed by White middle class rearing practice to give public verbal performances with strangers. Among older children and students coming from nonwhite working class backgrounds there may also be an awareness of the fact that testing has been and it is likely to be used as a vehicle of discrimination. It would be unrealistic to deny that this awareness and the

---

[17]Darlene F. Williams, "Black English and the Stanford-Binet Test of Intelligence," Stanford, CA: Stanford University School of Education, Ph.D. Thesis, 1979.

[18]A.V. Cicourel, et al., *Language Use and School Performance*, NY: Academic Press, 1974.

students' total perception of the testing situation will influence the pupils' testing behavior and the outcome of the tests.

Our comments on the possible bias of the reading tests examined in this article are based primarily on linguistic and cultural differences between working class Black English speakers and the White middle class language envisaged by the tests. The reason for this focus is that working class Black English speakers are probably proportionately the largest group exposed to the types of test bias discussed here. However, the principles illustrated by this discussion are applicable to test bias against other socioeconomic, cultural, and ethnic groups.

Specific Types of Language-Related Bias In Tests

In general, differences in language and culture might result in several types of bias in tests. Specifically, we shall discuss phonological, syntactic, and lexical bias. Most of the test items were selected from old editions of tests which are not specifically cited in order not to single out any one publisher for what are rather universal examples of bias in tests.

Phonological Bias

Many reading tests discriminate directly against bilingual/bidialectal speakers by asking them to distinguish among items which are homophones in their speech. The validity of this type of item is questionable. For example, Melmed[19] has demonstrated that Black children have additional homophones in their speech that speakers of mainstream dialect do not have but that this aspect of Black phonology does not interfere with the students' comprehension. As Shuy[20] has stated:

> Urban disadvantaged Negroes [sic] should not find it difficult to discover that /jes/ is realized in print as **just**. Their grapheme rule would be ‹st› - /s/ in final position. This is certainly no more unreasonable than other double grapheme relations as single sounds, such as ‹th› - /θ/ in **thin** or ‹mb› - /m/ in **thumb**. That is, the decoding process or reading is already imbued with such rules.

Since phonology need not interfere with comprehension, it does not seem valid to have students discriminate between very similar words out of context

---

[19]Paul Melmed, *Black English Phonology: The Question of Reading Interference*, Berkeley, CA: Language Behavior Research Laboratory, February 1970.

[20]Roger W. Shuy, "A Linguistic Background for Developing Beginning Reading Materials for Black Children," *Teaching Black Children to Read*, ed. Joan Baratz and Ralph W. Fasold, Washington, DC: Center for Applied Linguistics, 1969, p. 122.

as some indication of "reading" proficiency. This is particularly true when words that in the speech variety of specific regional or cultural groups are homophones of the correct choice are deliberately used as distractors.

Two problems are created by the use of this type of item: First, the teacher is led to assume that the phonology of the Black child is incorrect. In typical achievement tests, some 33% of the items can be "dialect preju-diced"[21]. The teacher must assume, when given the results of such a test, that the Black child has an incorrect phonological system.

Second, this type of item can contribute to the mistaken notion that, because sound-symbol relations for children who speak non-mainstream dialects may be different from those of other children, a phonic-linguistic, or decoding, approach to the teaching of reading is not useful for them. Such a conclusion can deprive these children of a successful approach for teaching them to read.[22][23][24][25][26][27][28][29] There has been some evidence showing that a phonic-linguistic method in which teachers teach the spelling patterns of English but accept the children's pronunciation is successful in teaching Black children to read.[30]

Many of the tests have subtests designed to measure pupils' knowledge of sound-letter relationships or skill in decoding. Students are asked to identify a dictated word from among several words. The following are possible homophones for dialect speakers, e.g. Black speakers, Southern

[21]J.O. Hutchinson, "Reading Tests and Nonstandard Language,"*Reading Teacher*, vol. 25, No. 5, February 1972, pp. 430-437.

[22]Jean Chall, *Learning to Read: The Great Debate*, NY: MacGraw-Hill, 1967.

[23]Rudolph Flesch, *Why Johnny Still Can't Read*, NY: Harper & Row, 1981.

[24]John Guthrie, S. Jay Samuels, et. al., A Study of the Locus and Nature of Reading Problems in the Elementary School," Final Report for National Institute of Education, Newark, DE: International Reading Association, 1976.

[25]Mary R. Hoover, "Characteristics of Black Schools at Grade Level: A Description," *Reading Teacher*, Vol. 31, No. 7, April 1978, pp. 757-762.

[26]Mary R. Hoover, Robert L. Politzer, and Shirley Lewis, "A Semi-Foreign Language Approach to Teaching Reading to Bidialectal Students," *Applied Linguistics and Reading*, ed. R. Shafer, Newark, DE: International Reading Association, 1979.

[27]Barak Rosenshine, "Notes on 'Successful' Programs in Compensatory Reading Education," Urbana, IL, University of Illinois Press, 1972, pp. 177-186.

[28]D. Skailand, "A Comparison of Four Language Units in Teaching Reading," Berkeley, CA; Language Behavior Research Laboratory, 1970.

[29]George Weber, *Inner City Children Can be Taught to Read*, Washington, DC: Council for Basic Education, 1972.

[30]Mary R. Hoover and Robert L. Politzer, "An Experiment in Teaching Reading to Bidialectical Children," Stanford, CA: Stanford Center for Research and Development in Teaching, #2, 1972.

speakers, Appalachian speakers, Latino speakers, which, if used in tests, may result in biased test items. (Rules included in Figure 1[31] [32] [33])

FIGURE 1
Sources of Potential Phonological Test Bias

Analysis	Example

Possible homophones: **had, hat**
Rule: At the end of a syllable, voiced stops;
    "b", "d" and "g" are pronounced as
    voiceless stops "p", "t" and "k".
Group Disadvantaged: Blacks

☐ had
☐ hat
☐ hate

Possible homophones: **held, helm**
Rule: Consonant clusters reduced when both members
    of the cluster are voiced or voiceless.
Groups Disadvantaged: Southerners
                      Blacks (nonstandard)

☐ held
☐ help
☐ head
☐ helm

Possible homophones: **this, these**
Rule: Lack of contrast between the two /i/ phonemes;
    devoicing of final consonants.
Group Disadvantaged: Latinos

☐ his
☐ those
☐ this
☐ these

Possible homophones: **tap, tab**
Rule: At the end of syllable, voiced stops "b",
    "d" and "g" are pronounced as voiceless stops
    "p", "t" and "k".
Group Disadvantaged: Blacks

☐ tag
☐ tape
☐ tap
☐ tab

Possible homophones: **right, rat**
Rule: Vowel glide "ay" often pronounced as in
    "sahd tahm"
Groups Disadvantaged: Southerners,
                       Blacks

☐ ripe
☐ right
☐ rat
☐ eight

---

[31]Ronald Williams and Walter Wolfram, *Social Dialects: Differences vs Disorders*, Rockville, MD; Speech and Hearing, 1977.

[32]Diana Bartley and Robert L. Politzer, *Practice Centered Teaching Training: Standard English for Speakers of Nonstandard Dialects*, Philadelphia, PA: Center for Curriculum Development, 1972.

[33]Geneva Smitherman, *Talkin' and Testifyin'*, Boston: Houghton Miflin Company, 1977.

Possible homophones: **tag, tack**
Rule: Same as Rule for "tap" above
Groups Disadvantaged: Blacks,
                               Latinos

☐ talk
☐ tack
☐ tag
☐ take

Possible homophones: **fur, for**
Rule: Loss of phonemic contrast before "r".
Groups Disadvantaged: Southerners,
                               Blacks
Note: In this instance, homophones are created for most
        in that **fare** and **fair** are also homophones for
        most speakers.

☐ fur
☐ fare
☐ for
☐ fair

Syntactic Bias

Some of the syntactic patterns in the tests examined are biased because the forms used are "superstandard," that is, worded in an elaborated, stylized format rather than a simple, standard English format.[34] For example, in one test, the sentence "only the person to whom you make it out" is used and the phrase "however, in and of itself" is used in another item. Labov[35] has demonstrated that such constructions often carry **less** information than nonstandard forms. The directions to a comprehension test say that it "measures the students' ability to read complete prose passages with understanding." Yet these complete prose passages are written primarily in a form of language which discriminates against working class children.

Some subtests which are not reading tests per se should also be mentioned because performance on these tests is likely to affect teachers' judgment concerning pupils' general performance in language arts. For example, a language expression subtest on one of the tests is supposed to test "how well you can use the language to express yourself." What it actually does is assess how well students can discriminate between standard and vernacular English. The children are asked to identify specific structures as wrong:

> They **sees** Rosa.
> **Don't never** use too much.
> You **done** it wrong.
> Mother didn't let me eat **no** candy.

---

[34]Ralph Fasold, *"Sloppy Speech in Standard English," paper read at the Fourth Triennial Conference on Symbolic Processes, Washington, DC: April 27, 1972.*
[35]*Labov, "Logic of Nonstandard . . ."*

Though the ability to distinguish between standard and vernacular English is a skill which correlates with reading achievement,[36] it is no more related to "using language well to express yourself" than vernacular English is. The misnomer "language expression" for a discrimination task is an excellent example of the general lack of validity in the language tests we have examined.

An oral comprehension subtest in which students are asked a series of questions on a poem uses the negative formation "neither you nor I." This formation would be superstandard to most children; awkward to many White nonstandard speakers, who form negatives differently; and foreign to many Blacks, who use a variety of negative formations still further from the superstandard norms. In addition, the form of the poem is culturally alien to many working class children. Black poetry, by contrast,[37] is rather concerned with stylistic devices such as sounding, shouting, and teaching.

Certain formats in tests also constitute a kind of syntactic bias. For example, the cloze format, used in many reading tests (e.g. the Gates-MacGinitie Reading Test, the Florida Teacher Certification Examination (reading subtest), is a very efficient way of finding out whether the modes of communication are the same as those of the test maker. However, it may be difficult to determine to what extent performance on cloze tests indicates comprehension rather than test bias. Some researchers assert that the cloze test format may be an unfair measure of the reading ability of a dialect speaker[38] [39] or a student with a field-dependent cognitive style[40] — particularly one who is "less academically gifted."[41]

---

[36]Robert L. Politzer and Mary R. Hoover, *"The Development of Awareness of the Black Standard/Black Nonstandard Dialect Contrast Among Primary School Children: A Pilot Study,"* Stanford, CA: Stanford Center for Research and Development in Teaching, February 1972.

[37]C. Rodgers, *"Black Poetry — Where it's At," Rappin' and Stylin' Out,* ed. T. Kochman, Urbana, IL: University of Illinois Press, 1972, pp. 177-186.

[38]Charles W. Bonds, "The Cloze Procedure and Dialect Considerations," *Clearing House,* Vol.50, April 1977, pp. 360-362.

[39]Mary R. Hoover, "Teacher Competency Tests as Educational Genocide for Blacks: The Florida Teacher Certification Exam.," *Negro Educational Review,* Vol. 35, No. 2, April 1984, pp. 70-74.

[40]C. Stansfield and J. Hansen, "Field Dependence-Independence as A Variable in Second Language Cloze Test Performance, *TESOL Quarterly,* Vol. 17, No. 1, 1983, pp. 29-38.

[41]L. Hansen, "Field Dependence-Independence and Language Testing: Evidence from Six Pacific Island Cultures," *TESOL Quarterly,* Vol. 18, No. 2, June 1984, pp. 311-324.

Carroll[42] has stated that the cloze format, more than other multiple-choice formats, depends on inference, which is not a "pure" measurement of comprehension.[43] As has been stated elsewhere[44]:

> Students from a culture in which inference is often couched in proverbial usage based on an African-oriented world view Alleyne calls "inversion" may not be as familiar with European styles of inference as traditional students.

Syntactic bias can also occur in the wording of instructions as illustrated by the following: In multiple choice items, testees are often asked to respond to instructions asking them to pick a correct statement from a group of incorrect ones. The instructions state that "none of the following are true except. . ." This kind of wording is probably confusing for anybody regardless of ethnic or social background (this was documented by one of the authors of this article by interviewing a large number of informants). The problem is that the fact that the one response that is correct is described by a negation ("except") of a negation ("None"). But for speakers of various speech varieties — especially Blacks — the "double" negation (or negation of a negation) is simply an emphatic negative: "**None** of the following is true except" is likely to be interpreted as "very definitely all of the following are false."

Lexical Bias

Students may fail an item in a test because they (1) are unfamiliar with a word because of class or geographical difference, (2) have a different orientation to or interpretation of the item, or, (3) possess information that is so similar to what the item requires as to prove confusing. In each of these cases, students may respond incorrectly to an item — not because they can't read, or because they are emotionally disturbed or perceptually handicapped — but because they have a different lexicon from that of the examiner. Examples of the above categories are as follows:

(1) unfamiliarity - "Point to the picture of the toboggan," (a person from South Florida may not know what a toboggan looks like apart from unfamiliarity with the word);

(2) different interpretation - "Is this a picture of a house?" (if a picture of a high rise housing project building is shown, an inner city testee might say "yes", while the test might presume "no" since the stereotyped story-book house is a single, detached unit);

[42]John B. Carroll, telephone interview, Chapel Hill, NC, August 10, 1983.

[43]John B. Carroll, "Defining Language Comprehension: Some Speculations," *Language Comprehension and the Acquisition of Knowledge*, ed. Carroll and R.O. Freedle, NY: John Wiley & Sons, 1972.

[44]Hoover, "Teacher Competency Tests. . ."

(3) similar information - "Are trains the only things that run on tracks?" (some urban dwellers may say "no" since subways and "els" also run on tracks, while the test may presume "yes").

Bias is also reflected in the word choices of the comprehension and vocabulary sections of most of the tests, and middle-class values are assumed. For example, one comprehension subtest has 34 paragraphs with pictures, of which only few have working class content. In a vocabulary subtest, students are asked to respond to the following:

If a person does something against the law, he is an:

ambassador	official
offender	officer

The answer could be not only "offender" but also "officer" for working class children who may have witnessed or otherwise experienced incidents of brutality, graft, and corruption involving police in their neighborhoods.

On a vocabulary subtest, students are asked to select the best synonym for inequality. Of the responses (absence, foreign, difference, similarity, and poor); all except "absence" and "similarity" could be "correct" in cultures in which students are aware that difference, poverty, and foreignness are associated with inequality.

Another form of bias in vocabulary is evidenced in the middle class style of most of the items. Hymes[45] elaborated a concept of language which includes not only the code, i.e. the phonology and syntax, mentioned in previous sections, but also the form and the topic of the message. Working class/bidialectal communities are known to have distinct forms of styles of the "message." Mitchell-Kernan[46] and Smitherman[47] have described a variety of speech events in the Black community from "sounding" to "rapping." Johnston[48] has described how these speech events affect the testing process for Black children. Most of these speech events affect the testing process for Black children. Most of these speech events contain a heightened use of metaphor.[49] One test item asks a child to pick the "right answer" in the following selection:

---

[45]Dell Hymes, "Toward Ethnographies of Communication: The Analysis of Communicative Events," *Language and Social Context*, ed. Pier Giglioli, Baltimore, MD: Penguin, 1972.

[46]Claudia Mitchell-Kernan, *Language Behavior in a Black Urban Community*, Berkeley, CA: Language Behavior Research Laboratory, February 1971.

[47]Smitherman, *Talkin'* . . .

[48]P. Johnston, "Prior Knowledge and Reading Comprehension Test Bias," *Reading Research Quarterly*, Vol. 19, 1984, pp. 219-239.

[49]A. Ortony *et. al.*, "Cultural and Instructional Influences on Figurative Language Comprehension by Inner City Children," *Research in Teaching of English*, Vol. 19, February 1985, pp. 5-36.

Father said: Once there was a land where boys and girls never grew up. They were always growing. What was Father telling?

The truth _____ A lie _____ A story _____

The "right" answer could be any of them. Metaphorically, it could be the "truth" if the growth were mental and not physical. It could be a "lie" in that the word "lie" in black speech can also mean a joke or a story, and it could also be "a story."

Other examples follow:

The hummingbird has a long slender bill. It thrusts this bill into flowers to get nectar and insects. When **15** it beats its wings so rapidly that they sound like the **16** of a tiny motor.

| 15 | = hopping | resting | flying | flowers | walking |
| 16 | = hum | scratch | grit | size | crash |

"Hum" or "crash" might be suitable responses for metaphorically sensitive children. On the same test, another item is ambiguous:

In ordinary **50**, the qualities of the speaker's voice give important clues to his thoughts and feelings. But when you read someone else's written work, you must study the **51** carefully so that you can interpret the **52** thoughts and feelings.

50	= textbooks	thinking	feelings	material	conversation
51	= dictionary	letters	text	syllables	spelling
52	= enthusiastic	common	listener's	writer's	association

The answer to number 52 could be "enthusiastic" as well as "writer's", (that one should withhold enthusiasm in the absence of any specific justification for it is probably a culture based judgment).

Speed was necessary, and Fred had tried to find a short cut through the forest. Now he knew that his **38** had not been a good one. He was **39**. More time than he could have saved would not be **40** trying to get his bearing.

38	= purchase	safe	time	decision	speed
39	= lost	large	asleep	torn	last
40	= saved	lockes	spent	clocked	sent

The answer could be, for **39**, "torn," "asleep," or "lost." (See Hill on figurative language used in reading tests.[50])

---

[50]Clifford Hill and Eric Larsen, "What Reading Tests Call For and What Children Do," NY: Program in Applied Linguistics, Teachers College, Columbia University, Final Report for National Institute of Education, Oct. 1983, p. 4-70-72.

Many items used in the selected tests are archaic, uncommon, and class-tied, representing superstandard, rather than standard vocabulary. The words are often relevant to no group, constituting almost a "new genre for English"[51]; they are particularly inappropriate for working-class children. For example, the word "chandelier" is used in one primary school vocabulary subtest, and is an example of a superstandard vocabulary item, particularly familiar to middle and upper classes. (What we are not endorsing here, however, that children should not acquire a wide vocabulary. What we are endorsing is the distribution of items across classes and cultures.) Several studies[52] [52] have demonstrated that mainstream Whites do poorly on tests geared to the vocabulary and cultures of Blacks and Appalachians. (If joint exposure is not possible, students should at least be exposed to the most generally used terms in the society at large rather than superstandard English.)

A final type of vocabulary bias is seen in the reading methodology featured. All of the tests selected for our discussion are geared to the student who has been taught with a sight approach to reading. All of the selections in the primary tests contain words selected on the same basis as words used in the sight approach textbooks — frequency of usage. Obviously, children taught with one of the phonic-linguistic approaches, e.g. Lippincott, Sullivan Programmed Reading, could be disadvantaged in that the reading method they have been exposed to uses words selected on the basis of spelling pattern "regularity." That bias is particularly severe for students in the first two grades. By the third grade, the student taught by a phonic-linguistic approach has been exposed to most English spelling patterns, and, therefore, is more likely to compete successfully with the student taught by a sight approach. This bias is particularly insidious because, as mentioned earlier, there is some evidence that a phonic-linguistic or decoding approach is one of the more successful approaches to teaching beginning reading skills to bidialectal speakers.

Consequences of Biases

The earliest tests used for educational purposes were developed in the 1920s with substantial support from corporate foundations. They were IQ tests based on Army Alpha tests used to assign soldiers to various tasks. The

[51]C. Fillmore, "Ideal Readers and Real Readers," *Analyzing Discourse: Text and Talk*, ed. D. Jannen, Washington, DC: Georgetown University Press, pp. 248-270.

[52]Robert L. Williams, "The Silent Mugging of the Black Community," *Psychology Today*, May 1974.

[53]Sol Adler, *Poverty Children and Their Language: Implications for Teaching and Testing*. NY: Grimes and Walton, Inc., 1979.

tests were used to identify individuals having the values, morality, and skills deemed appropriate for certain occupations. Other tests, including reading tests, are used for the same sorting purposes. To the extent that the sorting disproportionately places one group at a disadvantage to another, we can call it a form of political bias.

A form of this political bias can be seen in the use of tests for placement of students in reading groups. This "placement" often amounts to a tracking system in which low-income children are effectively "typed" as low or slow readers for life. As Rist[54] has demonstrated, children are often labeled "slow" in kindergarten, and they remain fixed in that category indefinitely. Because the teachers use the scores as a self-fulfilling prophecy, the students may never be taught adequately. Denied basic reading skills, these children become functional illiterates, adults unable to pass employment or college entrance tests, and thus are channeled into the ranks of the unemployed of which members of minority groups make up a disproportionate percentage.

Another example of political bias, or the use of tests that give one group an advantage over another, is seen in the use of various criterion-referenced tests to determine who graduates from high school and who doesn't.[55] The school is an educational enterprise that involves teachers, administrators, and students. The school fails in one of its endeavors — to teach its students literacy skills. Of the contributors to the failure, one group is singled out for penalty. Not the group that failed to teach. Not the group that failed to administer a successful school (see [56] [57] [58] [59] for details on success). No, the group singled out to suffer is the group that had least responsibility for the failure — the students.

The point here is not that there should be no standards. Students must be literate in order to cope with our highly technological society and to participate meaningfully in the democratic process. Where tests are used to penalize one group and not all participants in the educational act, however, political bias exists and should be eliminated.

---

[54]R. Rist, "Student Social Class and Teacher Expectations," *Challenging The Myths: The Schools, the Blacks and the Poor*, Cambridge, MA: Harvard Educational Review, 1971.

[55]Grann Lloyd, "Functional Literacy and/or Minimum Competency Testing in the Nation's Schools as a Prerequisite to Receiving a High School Diploma: Some Economic Implications," *Negro Educational Review*, Vol. 31, No. 1, January 1980, pp. 3-16.

[56]Weber, *Inner*...

[57]Hoover, "Characteristics..."

[58]Ronald Edmonds, "Effective Schools for the Urban Poor," *Educational Leadership*, Vol. 37, 1979, pp. 15-24.

[59]Irving McPhail, "A Critical Evaluation of George Weber's Classic Study of Schools Where Low-Income Minority Children Read at Grade Level," In Gentile, L. M. *et. al.* (ed's). *Reading Research Revisited.* Columbus, Ohio: Charles E. Merrill, 1983.

The elimination of test bias will not remove societal biases or societal value judgment concerning the superiority of one language variety over another. However, cultural or linguistically biased tests reinforce undesirable attitudes and give them the appearance of reflecting measurable scientific objectivity; society at large assumes that speakers of certain language varieties are likely to have lower scholastic achievement and the tests "prove" it. The tragedy is that few individuals — most specifically, teachers and pupils — realize that the "prove" is based on circular evidence: The communication styles and language of an ethnic group and/or social class are generally assumed to be "worse" that those of another and thus are not utilized in tests. The result is that the test performance of speakers of the excluded language variety is "worse."

The sad fact is that both teachers and pupils seem to learn to well the lesson that is taught by the tests. Research shows that teachers' expectations of pupils and judgments of pupils' potential are heavily influenced by speech style.[60] [61] [62] A study of teachers' and pupils' language attitudes conducted at the Stanford Center for Research and Development[63] demonstrated that teachers rate speakers of nonstandard Black English varieties as less likely to succeed in school than speakers of standard Black English. The Black pupils of these same teachers concurred with their teachers' judgments. Within the framework of this presentation, we need not go into a detailed discussion as to what this shared teacher/pupil judgement implies in a self-fulfilling hypothesis on the part of the teachers and in lowered expectation and self-concepts on the part of pupils. What is relevant to our discussion is that the mantle of scientific objectivity needs to be removed from tests which, because of bias in their construction, appear to confirm the association of low reading achievement with specific language varieties.

---

[60]F. Williams, "Some Research Notes on Dialect Attitudes and Stereotypes," *Language Attitudes: Current Trends and Prospects*, ed. Roger W. Shuy and Ralph W. Fasold, Washington, DC: Georgetown University Press, 1973, pp. 113-128.

[61]G.P. Seligman, G.R. Tucker, and W.E. Lambert, "The Effects of Speech Style and Other Attributes on Teacher Attitudes toward Pupils," *Language and Society*, Vol. 1, 1972, pp. 131-142.

[62]Orlando Taylor, "Teachers' Attitudes toward Black and Nonstandard English as Measured by the Language Attitude Scale," *Language Attitudes*, ed. Roger Shuy and Ralph Fasold, Washington, DC: Georgetown University, 1973.

[63]Robert L. Politzer and Mary R. Hoover, "Teachers and Pupil's Attitudes Toward Black English Speech Varieties and Black Pupils' Achievement," Stanford, CA: Stanford Center for Research and Development in Teaching, 1976.

Some Suggestions For Reducing Language and Culture Related Bias

What are some solutions to linguistic and cultural bias in reading tests? Do we:

(1) Throw out tests?
(2) Revise test content?
(3) Revamp a biased society?

With regards to the first option, achievement tests, or other forms of nationally normed tests, less biased than existing ones, are needed for at least one purpose: accountability to parents. Often the only means that parents have of assessing the performance of the school is the availability of achievement scores published annually in the newspaper.

A second important rationale for testing is the placement of children within a particular curriculum and reading series. Some schools have adopted simple end-of-book tests in their reading series as the major means of assessment for placement. Some of the state criterion-referenced tests are also based on skills which are actually taught.

We have stated, however, that most achievement and diagnostic tests are not designed to perform either of the above-stated functions. They do not do an adequate job of assessment for accountability because of bias in form and content, but they also do not do an adequate job of placement either because the diagnostic results are often not tied to a specific prescription or reading series.

If elimination of tests is not a viable solution, then it is the bias in the tests and not the tests which must be eliminated. A variety of means should be explored for the elimination of language-related test bias. One first step would be to treat specific examples of test bias mentioned in this presentation as hypotheses to be tested in controlled experiments. Objective reading tests could be examined carefully by sociolinguists and/or cultural anthropologists who could identify the biased items. We have stated above that this task would be relatively easy with the portions of the tests in which specific subskills of reading are being tested rather than reading itself. The tests could then be administered to groups of pupils speaking various language varieties. Assignment of pupils to a specific language variety group would have to be undertaken on the basis of specific and controlled oral language testing. The task would be complex, but not insurmountable, e.g. a test of dominance in Black vernacular over Black standard English was developed[64] at the Stanford Center for Research and Development in Teaching. The data

---

[64]Mary R. Hoover, D. Brown, S. Lewis, S. Hicks, R. Politzer, "Black English Tests for Students, Stanford, CA: Center for Educational Research at Stanford, 1976 (ERIC #ED-160-204).

obtained through administering the reading tests would then be examined in order to confirm or reject the sociolinguists' or anthropologists' hypotheses linking test bias with specific items. The items which "discriminate" (both in the technical as well as popular meaning of the word) could be rewritten or possibly eliminated from the tests. An alternative would be to examine from the scores and norms characterizing a specific group those items which have been determined to "discriminate." The latter may have some disadvantages, however: (1) unnecessary exposure of students to biased test items and (2) difficulty of assigning reliably large numbers of students to specific linguistic and/or cultural groups.

If new, unbiased reading tests are to be constructed, validity should be the first consideration. Reading is the decoding of and the extraction of meaning from a written or printed message. Tests of discrimination between sounds, and other real or presumed component skills of reading, may have some diagnostic value but they have no place in achievement testing. Many tests, especially those used at the lower levels, appear to confuse the diagnostic and achievement goals of testing. The two functions should become clearly separated. Diagnostic tests of tests of component skills should be made as linguistically fair as possible according to suggestions made above (e.g. elimination of items that are found to be discriminatory). Achievement testing could then focus on the testing of reading rather than component skills. While "comprehension" and its testing are debatable subjects, there are methods of testing pupils' comprehension of a written message which have relatively high face validity. Some of these methods have been employed in foreign language testing for some time, but they seem equally valid in testing reading comprehension in the native tongue. Among these methods are: (1) carrying out of an instruction that has been given in written form, (2) judging whether statements are true or false according to a **short** paragraph that the examinee has just read, and (3) writing a short paraphrase of written material.

Vocabulary, which has been estimated to constitute a major component of comprehension (Davis[65]), also provides a relatively unbiased assessment of reading comprehension[66]. Though vocabulary items can be reflective of certain classes and geographical areas, they are less subject to the ambiguity, lack of validity, and trickery that is often characteristic of multiple choice "comprehension" items.

---

[65]Frederick Davis, "Research in Comprehension in Reading," *Reading Research Quarterly*, Vol. 3, No. 4, Summer 1968, pp. 507-545.

[66]Mary R. Hoover, "A Culturally Appropriate Approach to Teaching Basic Communication Skills to Black College Students," *Negro Educational Review*, January 1982, 32, 14-27.

subject to the ambiguity, lack of validity, and trickery that is often characteristic of multiple choice "comprehension" items.

Some of the older diagnostic reading tests (Spache's Diagnostic Reading Scales, Gates-McKillop Reading Diagnostic Tests), used primarily by remedial reading teachers, provide examples of oral reading assessment which can be utilized in fair and valid instruments. Students are asked to read orally paragraphs which are timed and followed by oral comprehension questions. This format has the advantage of minimizing misunderstanding about directions. A disadvantage is that the items have to be administered individually to students. The Nairobi Method[67] [68] combines a brief oral and written assessment for a full diagram of reading composition and research skills for college students, and is an example of a relatively unbiased assessment for minority students.

Whatever the diagnosis and program, the ultimate goal of instruction must be that children who come from a linguistic background unlike that of the White middle class learn to read the same English and pass the same tests as all others. We doubt that many people, especially the parents of those children, would want it otherwise. That this goal is not unreasonable is demonstrated by the existence (aforementioned) across the country of numbers of schools at which inner-city Black and other predominantly working class children read at grade level.

In conclusion, we must stress that the linguistic and cultural biases present in diagnostic or reading achievement tests are ultimately the reflections of **biases present** in the teaching process and in society as a whole.[69] While removing cultural and linguistic biases from tests is a laudable undertaking, we should remember that the final success of culture fair tests depends on the establishment of culture fair teaching in a culture fair society. Even the most biased diagnostic or pseudo-diagnostic test items discussed earlier have a certain **de-facto** validity if they are used to judge the student's progress in a culturally biased teaching process, i.e., whether a student has the same homonyms as the

[67]Mary R. Hoover and Robert L. Politzer, "A Culturally Appropriate Composition Assessment: The Nairobi Method," *Variations in Writing: Functional and Linguistic-Cultural Differences,* ed. M. Whiteman, Hillsdale, NJ: Lawrence Ehrlbaum, 1982, 197-208.

[68]Shirley Lewis, "Practical Aspects of Teaching Composition to Bidialectal Students: The Nairobi Method," *Variations in Writing: Functional and Linguistic-Cultural Differences,* ed. M. Whiteman, Hillsdale, NJ: Lawrence Ehrlbaum 1982, 189-196.

[69]Asa G. Hilliard, III, "Standardized Testing and African-Americans: Building Assessor Competence in Systematic Assessment," *Testing, Teaching and Learning: Report of a Conference on Research Testing,* ed. R. Tyler and S. White, Washington, D.C.: National Institute of Education, 1979.

speaker of a standard dialect is and should be irrelevant for his learning to read, but the student's performance on the items may become a good predictor of achievement if the student is exposed to teaching that rejects his/her pronunciation and confuses reading instruction with attempts to manipulate speech.

The existence of linguistic and cultural differences, which, according to our assumptions, is among the chief causes of test biases, is a societal fact. So is it true that variance exists in the prestige of speech varieties, that the more prestigious varieties dominate in the written medium and that the schools are obligated to teach the prestigious forms of language. The total removal of linguistic and cultural biases from tests may become possible only in the measure to which society removes the social stratifications which lead to linguistic cultural distances and sets about redefining its view of linguistic prestige. The attempt to remove linguistic and cultural bias from tests must be part of a larger process of reducing linguistic and cultural biases and their economic consequences.

Alternatives to Standardized Tests in Reading Education: Cognitive Styles and Informal Measures

by
Alice M. Scales

Standardized reading tests have been used to exclude, to retain, and to promote students in school. Usually, such test require the reading of passages and the answering of questions about the passages. Scores earned from answering questions are usually compared to scores earned by the tests' norm populations. Students who are better test-takers will score more like the higher-range norm populations for standardized tests than students who are poorer test-takers.

One reason may be that the cognitive styles of better test-takers' compare favorably with higher-range norm populations. Research[1] into the effect of cognitive styles on reading achievement has pointed out that reflective style students tend to score better on tests than impulsive style students. Evidently, their skill in responding to tests' questions merits them higher test scores.

Another reason some students may be better test-takers is that they may not have to read the test's passages to answer the questions. In their study where four diagnostic reading tests were used, Allington, Chodos, Domaracki, and Truex[2] found that subjects successfully answered one-fourth of the questions without reading the passages. Furthermore, they noted that the questions tended to measure factual knowledge moreso than comprehension skills. Tuinman[3] examined five standardized reading tests and found that none could be rated as having all passage dependent questions. Sidman and

[1]Isabelle B. King, "An Experimental Investigation of the Potential of Reflection-Impulsivity as a Determinant of Success in Early Reading Achievements" (Ph.D. dissertation, Boston College, 1972), Dissertation Abstracts International, 1972, vol. 33, no. 1-2, pp. 191A-192A; Judith Frances Lucas Lesiak, "The Relationship of Reflection-Impulsivity Dimensions and the Reading Ability of Elementary School Children at Two Grade Levels" (Ph.D. dissertation, Ohio State University, 1970). Dissertation Abstracts International, 1971, vol. 32, no. 1-2, p. 244A; Beryl Louis Johnson, "Conceptual Tempo and the Achievement of Elementary School Boys" (Ph.D. dissertation, Case Western Reserve University, 1969). Dissertation Abstracts International, 1970, vol. 30, no. 7-9, p. 3789A; and Jerome Kagan, "Reflection-Impulsivity and Reading Ability in Primary Grade Children," *Child Development*, vol. 36, no. 3 (1965), pp. 609-628.

[2]Richard L. Allighton, Laura Chodos, Jane Domaracki and Sharon Truex, "Passage Dependency: Four Diagnostic Oral Reading Tests," *The Reading Teacher*, vol. 30, no. 4, (January 1977), pp. 369-375.

[3]Jaap J. Tuinman, "Determining the Passage Dependency of Comprehension Questions in 5 Major Tests," *Reading Research Quarterly*, vol. 9, no. 2 (1973-1974), pp. 206-223.

Wilson-Morris[4] found that two-thirds of their subjects answered correctly ninety-six percent of the questions from a widely used aphasia test without reading the passages. Such being the case, it seems unnecessary for some students to have to read all of a test's passages in order to answer many of the test's questions. Using the data from such tests to exclude, to retain, and to promote students then may mean using data that could be misleading. Less misleading data may be obtained from using informal test designed to assess students' reading performance with classroom text material.

The purposes for this paper are to consider cognitive styles of students as they relate to test-taking and to describe informal reading measures that may be considered as alternatives to standardized reading tests.

Discussion

"Cognitive style is a general concept, referring to individual variation and preference in perceiving, remembering, and problem-solving."[5] Realization of students' individual variations and preferences assumes a recognition of their cognitive (reflective or impulsive) styles. Reflective style students will display high standards of performance as they take test or solve problems with few signs of thoughtlessness, whereas impulsive style students will display low standards of performance with little or no thought to the task at hand.

Irrespective of their cognitive style, students are expected to perform well on tests with established validity and reliability. (Validity indicates that a test measures what it claims to measure. Reliability determines that a test is consistent, over a period of time, in measuring whatever it measures). Even though standardized test have established validity and reliability, that does not ensure a totally accurate measure of students' reading skill. Passage independent questions on standardized tests have supported that contention. With the belief that standardized tests are nonexclusive for measuring reading skills of students, informal tests offer an alternative.

Because of the lack of established validity and reliability of informal measures, critics have argued against their value to determine grade place-

---

[4]Murray Sidman and Martha Wilson-Morris, "Testing for Reading Comprehension: A Brief Report on Stimulus Control," *Journal of Applied Behavior Analysis*, vol. 7, no. 2 (Summer 1974), pp. 327-332.

[5]Beth Davey, "Cognitive Styles and Reading Achievement." *Journal of Reading*, vol. 20, no. 2 (November 1976), pp. 113-120.

ment and their power to determine specific strengths and weaknesses.[6] Support for informal reading measures has been evident. Pikulski[7] noted that a strength of informal reading inventories lies in the close correspondence between the test material and the teaching material. Test material then, depending on the purpose for testing, could be different for each student. Therefore, consideration of establishing validity and reliability for informal reading measures becomes questionable and unnecessary.

Informal reading measures have included such instruments as the Informal Reading Inventory (IRI), the Reading Miscue Inventory (RMI), the Informal Reading Assessment Inventory (IRAI), the Cloze procedure, and the Maze procedure, all designed to determine profiles of students' reading performance. Even though there are differences among the measures, each is designed to involve variation in cognitive styles (reflective or impulsive) of students.

IRI. The IRI[8] is not one test. It is a test-design that permits test-developers (both commercial and classroom-teacher) to follow a general set of guidelines (develop vocabulary list, select passages to be read, and write questions for the passages) as they construct their tests. Vocabulary for the test may be words that the test-developer identifies as those that should be known by students at an identified school grade level. Selected reading passages may be taken from textbooks that have established reading levels. When reading levels of passages have not been established, readability formulae may be used to approximate the levels. Questions for IRIs are usually developed and written at the literal, inferential, and applicative levels. Grade levels within one constructed IRI may be for one grade level or for several grade levels.

The purposes for the IRI are to establish reading grade levels (independent, instructional, frustrational) and to identify strengths and weaknesses of word recognition and comprehension skills of students. Results from an IRI should correspond with test material found in the classroom. Commercial IRIs may not be as well suited for this task as teacher-developed ones. A major reason is that commercial IRIs can not be developed from text materials in individual classrooms. Authors of commercial IRIs attempt to

---

[6]Joe Peterson, M. Jean Greenlaw and Robert J. Tierney, "Assessing Instructional Placement with the IRI: The Effectiveness of Comprehension Questions," *The Journal of Educational Research*, vol. 71, no. 5 (May/June 1978), pp. 247-250; and Leo M. Schell and Gerald S. Hanna, "Can Informal Reading Inventories Reveal Strengths and Weaknesses in Comprehension Subskills?", *The Reading Teacher*, vol. 35, no. 3 (December 1981), pp. 263-268.

[7]John Pikulski, "A Critical Review: Informal Reading Inventories," *The Reading Teacher*, vol. 28, no. 2 (November 1974), pp. 141-151.

[8]Jean W. Gillet and Charles Temple. *Understanding Reading Problems: Assessment and Instruction* (Boston: Little, Brown and Company, 1982), pp. 87-101; 130-134.

use material that is general in scope. However, results from such IRIs may not transfer to individual classroom text material, whereas teacher-developed IRIs may be developed from materials that are used in the classroom. For example, if classroom teachers wanted to establish instructional reading levels for students of social studies textbooks in their classrooms, they could select 250 word passages from the beginning, middle, and end of the textbooks. For each passage, teachers would construct questions at the literal, inferential, and applicative levels. Teachers would also prepare separate copies of the passages to be used as their record for recording oral reading errors made by students. As students complete their reading of each passage, teachers ask them to respond orally to the questions. Scores based on the oral reading errors and the questioning errors are used to judge students' word recognition skill and to establish their reading levels.

Even though accuracy of IRIs is dependent upon the skill of IRI developers, IRIs have been used widely and are likely to remain a valuable measure for assessing students' reading performance.[9]

RMI. RMI[10] is an informal commercial test that was designed to examine

"...the way in which both language processes and thought processes function in the reading act...It can aid [in]...determin[ing] the varying causes of a reader's miscues [any deviation from the printed text], can pinpoint specific repetitive problems, and can distinguish them from difficulties which are caused by the organization or content of the reading material."[11]

Major components of the inventory are passages for students to read, copies of the passages to be used by teachers to record students' miscues, nine different questions for teachers to ask themselves about students' miscues, and profile charts. By far, the nine questions that relate to semantic acceptability, grammatical function, dialect, self correction, meaning change, grammatical acceptability, intonation, graphic similarity, and sound similarity seem to be the most important part of the inventory. They can be used to analyze miscues from passages other than the ones included in the inventory. Specifically, teachers could select passages from trade-books or textbooks. Irrespective of the source, passages should be difficult ones that students have not seen or heard before. Difficult passages are necessary so that students will miscue as they read. Goodman and Burke[12] indicated that at least 25 miscues should be recorded for analyzation of each passage.

[9]Jerry L. Johns and Mary K. Lunn, "The Informal Reading Inventory: 1910-1980," *Reading World*, vol. 23, no. 1 (October 1983), pp. 8-19.
[10]Yetta M. Goodman and Carolyn L. Burke. *Reading Miscue Inventory Manual* (New York: Macmillan Publishing Company, 1972).

students will miscue as they read. Goodman and Burke[12] indicated that at least 25 miscues should be recorded analyzation of each passage.

In the administration of the RMI, students are given difficult passages to read orally. Whenever they deviate from the text, their miscue is recorded by the teacher. Upon completion of a passage, students should be asked to retell as much of the passage as they can recall. Probing questions are permitted from the teacher after the student has exhausted his or her memory of the passage. Following the retelling, teachers then use the nine questions to analyze the miscues. Also, to determine the student's comprehension of the passage, his/her retelling script is compared to a passage outline that was teacher developed. Percentages of the miscues made and the substance of the retelling script are then used to identify students' reading strengths and reading weaknesses in sound/graphic relationships, grammatical relationships, and comprehension patterns.

IRAI. The IRAI[13] was designed to incorporate salient features from the IRI and the RMI. Reasons for the IRAI are that the IRI does not include provisions for a qualitative analysis of reading performance and the RMI is time consuming and difficult to interpret without prior training.

IRAI can be developed with difficult passages selected from such reading material as recreational, trade-book, content area, and instructional textbooks. Readability of the passages may be computed to approximate reading levels among the passages. A coding script of the passages should be prepared for the teacher. Criteria (e.g., problems to be solved, questions to be answered, directions for presenting concepts) that will determine the student's comprehension of the passages should be written. As the student reads that passage orally, miscues are recorded by the teacher. Student then responds to as much of the criteria as possible to determine his or her comprehension of the passages. Interpretation of the IRAI is accomplished by evaluating students responses to the comprehension criteria and by analyzing the miscues in the context of self-correct, graphic similarity, maintained meaning, and altered meaning. Such an analysis may suggest quickly whether students are perceiving, remembering, and problem-solving.

Unlike the IRI and like the RMI, grade level is not the concern. The concern is to determine how students process information as they read. For example, when students self-correct their miscues or substitute a meaningful word for the text-word, we know that they have involved themselves in the

---

[11]Ibid., p. 5.

[12]Ibid.

[13]Alice M. Scales, "The Informal Reading Assessment Inventory," *The Reading Instruction Journal*, vol. 24, no. 1 (Fall 1980), pp. 5-7.

language and thought processes of the passage. In other words, they have used their thought processes to influence their reading performance.

Cloze. Cloze[14] is an assessment procedure that can be used for placement and diagnostic purposes. An aim for placement is to determine whether a particular piece of written text represents a student's independent, instruction, or frustration reading level. An aim for diagnoses is to assess the quality of a student's use of context as a strategy for understanding what is read.[15]

Cloze tests may be constructed from various types of classroom material with passages of about 275 words. Passages should be typed. The first and the last sentences should remain intact. However, other sentences should have every fifth, eighth, or tenth word deleted. The deleted words should be replaced with equal length blank lines throughout the passage. Students are administered the test by directing them to read the passage and write in a missing word with whatever word they think was omitted. Only the exact omitted word can be accepted as correct. Approximately, 60% correct and up indicates an independent reading level, 40% to 60% indicates an instructional reading level, and below 40% indicates a frustrational reading level.

Cloze tests may be as reliable as standardized test. Results from Jones and Pikulski's[16] study indicated a significant relationship between cloze tests and standardized tests. Further, in an interview, Earl F. Rankin pointed out that the correlations between cloze and standardized tests tend to range from .70 to .80[17]. Also, cloze test offer an opportunity for analyzing the way students' use their language during the reading process. Similar to the RMI and the IRAI, cloze is not bound by a time factor; and the students' responses will indicate whether perceiving, remembering, and problem-solving have occurred as they read.

Maze. Maze is a modified cloze technique that may be designed to assess reading performance as it relates to reading levels. Guthrie, Seifert, Burnham, and Caplan[18] proposed the selection of passages that are new to

[14]Wilson Taylor, "Cloze Procedures: A New Tool for Measuring Readability," *Journalism Quarterly*, vol. 30, no. 4 (Fall 1953), pp. 415-433.

[15]Gillet and Temple, *Understanding Reading Problems: Assessment and Instruction*.

[16]Margaret B. Jones and John J. Pikulski, "Cloze for the Content Area Teacher," *Reading World*, vol. 18, no. 3 (March 1979), pp. 253-258.

[17]James D. Peebles, "An Interview with Earl F. Rankin on the Cloze Procedure" in *Reading and Writing: Concepts for Teaching and Learning*, pp. 51-62. Edited by Alice M. Scales and James D. Peebles. Pittsburgh: School of Education, University of Pittsburgh, Reprinted 1980.

[18]John T. Guthrie, Mary Seifert, Nancy A. Burnham, and Ronald I. Caplan, "The Maze Technique to Assess, Monitor Reading Comprehension," *The Reading Teacher*, vol. 28, no. 2 (November 1974), pp. 161-168.

students and that are about 120 words in length. Passages should be typed with every fifth word replaced with three alternative words. Alternatives should be typed with one word above the line, one word on the line, and one word below the line. Alternative words should include the correct word and two incorrect words. One incorrect word should be from the same grammatical class as the correct word. The other incorrect word should be from a different grammatical class than the correct word. For each maze, words should be alternated so that the correct word will change positions throughout the passage. Mazed passages are administered to students by teachers. Students read the passages, select one of the three words for an answer, and circle the answer.

Reading levels of the passages are determined in percentages. Students who perform at about 90% accuracy should be reading at their instructional level, 50 to 90% performance would be their instructional level, and below 50% would be their frustrational level.

Like cloze, as students read a maze passage, it becomes necessary for them to comprehend the semantic and syntactic structure of the passage in order to select the appropriate answer. Comprehension of maze passages may be illustrated as students demonstrate their ability to perceive, remember, and problem-solve.

Conclusions

Cognitive styles of the students will influence their reading performance as they work through informal tests. Seemingly, impulsive style students may have more of an advantage with informal tests than with standardized tests. Their tendency toward thoughtlessness as they perform reading tasks may be somewhat reduced as they become engaged in responding to evaluation criteria of various informal tests. For example, evaluation criteria for the IRAI may require that students diagram a concept after reading a passage or tell about the main points in the passage. With cloze, students will have to make sense from the passage in order to provide a missing word. Reflective style students' thoughtfulness, as they perform reading task, plus the content (classroom material) of informal reading test may ensure a more accurate reading performance profile for them than standardized reading test profiles. This assumption is related to the fact that many questions on standardized test are text independent, and reflective style students take advantage of passage independent questions by not reading the passages.

Recommendations

Practice in schools has been to rely on the results of standardized test to exclude, to retain, and to promote students in school. Research has disclosed flaws in standardized tests, thereby raising caution regarding educational decisions that are based on their results. When implemented, the following recommendations may provide some balance to standardized testing in classrooms: developing and using informal tests with students, analyzing standardized tests used in classrooms for assurance that they test reading skills, contrasting results from informal tests to results from standardized tests, and utilizing test results that are based on measuring reading performance to make educational decisions about students.

THE IMPACT OF TESTING ON AFRICAN AMERICANS

It's Time To Examine The Examiners

by
John G. Weiss

A generation after civil rights marches, legislation and litigation struck down the literacy tests that excluded millions of minorities from exercising their right to vote, evidence is mounting that tests are once again being used to unfairly deny Blacks and Hispanics access. This time the barriers are standardized admissions and licensing exams which are the gatekeepers to America's schools and occupations.

As former Educational Testing Service executive Chuck Stone recently told the New York State Legislature, "the testing industry has become America's cradle-to-grave arbiter of social mobility."[1] Each year, scores from over 40 million standardized multiple-choice tests alter the educational and career opportunities of millions of students and workers.[2]

Case Study: College Admissions Tests

Most of the nation's four-year colleges require the Scholastic Aptitude Test (SAT) or the American College Test (ACT) for admission. A survey by the College Board and the American Association of Collegiate Registrars and Admissions Officers found that more than forty percent of America's colleges automatically deny admission to applicants with test scores below arbitrary cut-off levels.[3] This presents a formidable barrier to Blacks and Hispanics whose SAT scores average 200 points below those of whites[4].

Reliance on test scores also systematically reduces the educational options for high school girls. The average difference between the sexes on the SAT is now at its largest gap ever — 61 points in favor of men[5]. Last year females scored 50 points lower on the Math section, and 11 points lower on the Verbal section. What makes this gap particularly worrisome is that although the SAT is supposed to predict first year college grades, research shows that women's first year grades, including their math grades, are higher than their male counterparts. If the SAT predicted equally well for both sexes, girls would score about 20 points higher than boys, rather than 61 points lower.

---

[1]Testimony by Chuck Stone before a special New York Legislative Committee hearing on extending Truth-in-Testing and Golden Rule reforms to professional licensing exams, May 20, 1986.
[2]A FairTest research project in progress has already found that at least 40 million standardized multiple-choice tests are administered each year in America.
[3]The American Association of Collegiate Registrars and Admissions Officers and the College Board, *Undergraduate Admissions*, 1980.
[4]SAT statistics from L. Ramist and S. Arbeiter, *Profiles of College Board Scores*, 1986.
[5]*The New York Times*, August 3, 1986.

Unfairly low SAT scores harm females and minorities in at least three ways, with minority females doubly penalized by both the gender and racial biases of the SAT. **(See Exhibit 1)**. First, unfairly low scores reduce their chances of gaining admission to colleges that rely heavily on the SAT. Second, unfairly low SAT scores reduce students' perceptions of their own ability. Carnegie Institute for the Advancement of Teaching President Ernest Boyer recently examined how test scores influence high school students' decisions about where they will apply to college. He found that over 60% of America's high school students lowered their educational aspirations after receiving their SAT or ACT test scores.[6]

Finally, low test scores reduce students' chances of obtaining grants or financial aid from numerous private and public foundations. In 1985, all recipients of college scholarships awarded by the state of Alabama were white, even though the public school system is nearly 50% minority. Information made public through a class action lawsuit revealed that the state's heavy reliance on ACT scores was the reason no minority students received scholarships.

Exhibit 1

MINORITY FEMALES: DOUBLE JEOPARDY

As the following chart documents, minority female high school students are doubly penalized by both gender and racial biases of the SAT. In every category, males outscore females:

	Females	Males	
Asian-Pacific Americans	897	946	-49 points
Black	705	748	-43 points
Mexican-Americans	775	845	-70 points
Native Americans	790	855	-65 points
Puerto Rican	744	820	-76 points
White	912	969	-57 points
National Average	877	938	-61 points

— from *1985 Profiles, College Bound Seniors*
by Leonard Ramist & Solomon Arbeiter, CEEB 1986.

---

[6]*The New York Times*, November 11, 1986.

Exhibit 2
OCCUPATIONS THAT REQUIRE
STANDARDIZED LICENSING TESTS
(partial list)

- Accountants
- Arborists
- Architects
- Attorneys
- Auto Mechanics
- Babcock Test Operators
- Barbers
- Blood Bank Specialists
- Boiler Engineers
- Chemists
- Certified Professional Accountants
- Chiropractors
- City Planners
- Cytotechnologists
- Dental Hygienists
- Dieticians
- Engineers
- Firefighters
- Foreign Service Officers
- Golf Pros
- Hairdressers
- Hearing Aid Dealers
- Hemotologists
- Insurance Adjusters
- Insurance Brokers
- Insurance Consultants
- Land Surveyors
- Medical Lab Technicians
- Medical Record Technicians
- Microbiologists
- Motion Picture Projectionists
- New York Stock Exchange Brokers
- Nurses
- Nursing Home Administrators
- Occupational Therapists
- Oil Burner Servicemen
- Optometrists
- Osteopathic Physicians
- Pest Control Operators
- Pesticide Applicators
- Physical Therapists
- Picture Framers
- Plumbers
- Podiatrists
- Police Officers
- Practical Nurses
- Professional Engineers
- Psychological Examiners
- Psychologists
- Radiologic Technologists
- Real Estate Brokers
- Real Estate Salesmen
- School Bus Operators
- School Teachers
- School Principals
- Securities Agents
- Securities Salesmen
- Sewage Treatment Operators
- Social Workers
- Veterinarians
- Welders

[7]*The Hartford Advocate*, November 3, 1986.

Number of boys and girls who obtained National Merit Scholarship cut-off scores in 1986:

State	Boys	Girls
California	817	493
Idaho	49	14
Massachusetts	305	178
New Jersey	324	173
New Mexico	66	24

The multi-million dollar National Merit Scholarship Program refuses to even consider students who do not achieve a certain cut-off score. While the National Merit Scholarship Program refuses to release racial or gender information on the students to whom they award over $30 million each year, a study in West Hartford, Connecticut, revealed that only 20% of the award recipients during the past 3 years were females.

Case Study: Teacher Testing

This year the scores from over ten million standardized tests will help determine who will — and who will not — be permitted to sell insurance, practice law, fight fires, work as nurses or enter nearly 100 other professions. (Exhibit 2). The growth of testing in the teaching profession illustrates the impact these exams are having on our society.

Exhibit 3

The WISC-R IQ Test

In 1971 Black parents in San Francisco filed a class action suit on behalf of their children who had been inappropriately labeled retarded by biased IQ tests, including America's largest selling intelligence test, the Wechsler Intelligence Scale for Children — Revised (WISC-R). It is published by The Psychological Corporation, a subsidiary of Harcourt Brace Jovanovich. In September 1986, in order to settle a class action lawsuit spearheaded by the Public Advocates law firm and the Association of Black Psychologists, the California Department of Education agreed to order school districts to stop administering the WISC-R and all other commercially available IQ tests to track Black children into classes for the educatably mentally retarded. The following are a few items from the WISC-R IQ test:

> 1) **What is the thing to do when you cut your finger?**
> **2 point response: Put a bandaid on it**
> **1 point response: Go to the hospital**
> **0 point response: Cry, bleed or suck on it**
> **—WISC-R IQ Test**

> *Minority children usually perform poorly on this item. A few years ago a Baltimore, Maryland sociologist asked several inner-city youths why they answered the question the way they did. She found that many of these kids answered "go to a hospital" because they thought that cut meant a big cut. Or they thought it was a small cut — and since they didn't have any bandaids at home, they answered "sucked on it" — and received no points.*

2) What is the thing to do if you lose a ball that belongs to one of your friends?
    2 point response: Buy him a new one and pay for it
    1 point response: Look all over for it, try to find it
    0 point response: I'd just cry, tell him you're sorry, apologize

                        —WISC-R IQ Test

If you're poor, it often is not possible to buy another one and it is unlikely that you have one to give. If the ball is really lost, looking for it is a waste of time. And if it is not really lost but could be found, wouldn't looking for it be more "intelligent" than buying a new one? Crying or apologizing might be the best response for a poor child, but such an answer will yield a lower "intelligence" score.

3) What are you supposed to do if you find someone's wallet or pocketbook in a store?
    2 point response: Return it
    1 point response: Give it to the store owner
    0 point response: Keep it; make believe you didn't see it

                        —WISC-R IQ Test

Is a poor hungry child really less intelligent if s/he keeps the money? Also a child — especially a minority child — might ignore the wallet/pocketbook for fear that s/he would be accused of stealing it. Such a response would earn the child no points.

Other WISC-R items include:
4 What are some reasons why we need policemen?
5 Why is it usually better to give money to a well-known charity than to a beggar?
6 From what country did America become independent in 1776?
7 Who discovered America?
8 What is the capital of Greece?
9 What are hieroglyphics?
10 Who was Charles Darwin?

STANDARDIZED COLLEGE AND
GRADUATE SCHOOL ADMISSION TESTS

- Achievement Tests
- Advanced Placement Tests
- Allied Health Entrance Examination
- Aptitude for Practical Nursing Examination
- Aptitude Test for Allied Health Programs
- American College Testing Program Exam
- College Achievement Tests
- Dental Admissions Tests
- Entrance Exam for Schools of Nursing
- Graduate Management Admissions Test
- Graduate Record Examination
- Law School Admissions Test
- Medical College Admissions Test
- Miller Analogies Test
- Optometry College Admissions Test
- Pharmacy College Admissions Test
- P.S.A.T./National Merit Scholarship Qualifying Exam
- Pre-Entrance Nursing Aptitude Battery
- Test of English as a Foreign Language
- Veterinary Aptitude

During the past decade, over 40 states have mandated that individuals seeking to enter the teaching profession must pass a standardized multiple-choice test.[8] According to a 1986 study by University of Florida Professor G. Pritchy Smith, the combined impact of these exams will drastically reduce the number of minority college graduates entering teaching.[9]

*Since 1978 in Louisiana, only 15 percent of the Black teacher candidates compared to 78 percent of the white candidates passed the National Teacher Examination (NTE) which is required for initial certification.

*The differential in pass rates for whites and minorities on Florida's Teacher Certification Examination (92 percent for whites; 37 percent for Blacks; 57 percent for Hispanics) is a significant factor in Florida's certification of only 200 Blacks out of a total of 5,500 new teachers, a Black representation of just 3.6 percent.

---

[8]G. Pritchy Smith, 'Unresolved Issues and New Developments in Teacher Competency Testing', *Urban Educator*, Fall 1986.
[9]*Ibid*.

*In Texas, the existing disproportionate representation of minority educators is likely to be greatly exacerbated in the future as a result of use of the Pre-Professional Skills Test (PPST), which is a new requirement for applicants to teacher training programs. Projections from the Texas data indicate that Blacks will constitute only about 1.7 percent and Hispanics only about 6 percent of the annual graduating class of certified teachers in that state.[10]

*Use of standardized tests will reduce Black representation among teachers being certified in Alabama to 5%; in Arizona to 2%; in California to 2%; in Connecticut to 0.7%; in Georgia to 6.7%; in Oklahoma to 1.5%; and in Virginia to 2.7%.

This data suggests a deepening crisis. Not only does a decline in minority representation in teaching represent decreased access to this important profession for minority adults, it also robs students of role models during their formative years. The American Association of Colleges for Teacher Education (AACTE) projects that, by 1990, minority teachers will comprise only 6 percent of the teaching population, while nearly 40% of America's public school population will come from minority backgrounds.[11]

Shaping Our Expectations

Tests are obviously powerful gatekeepers. But they have another very powerful effect on those who take them. The seemingly scientific aura surrounding standardized tests often causes individuals to internalize these measures. Study after study shows the 'Pygmalion' effect: expectations lead to fulfillment. Once students are tracked into low-level groups, the test's assessment of their abilities becomes a self-fulfilling prophecy. Michigan State Education Professor Diana Pullin concludes that: "The diluted curriculum and instruction provided in the lower levels leaves the students enrolled there further and further behind their age peers, rather than enhancing their attainment so that they might catch up. The result of test use to determine class placement, therefore, often serves as a roadblock to future educational opportunities."[12]

For large numbers of minority youth, failure to pass a multiple-choice high school graduation test bars entry into the job market, even into military service. Furthermore, as Dr. George Madaus, Director of the Center for Testing and Evaluation at Boston College has stated, the prospect of the loss

---

[10]*Ibid.*
[11]*Ibid.*
[12]Diana Pullin, 'Educational Testing: Impact on Children at Risk', *NCAS Backgrounder*, vol. 1, no. 2.

of a diploma even after twelve years of the requisite attendance and passing grades has apparently been daunting enough to provoke an increase in the rate of school dropouts.[13]

For those minority students who have overcome innumerable social and economic barriers and achieved academic success in early schooling, the denial of access to higher education because of low college or graduate school admissions test scores is particularly frustrating. Many law schools place twice as much weight on the LSAT as on a student's undergraduate grade point average. This means academic achievements built up over four years may be torn down in just four hours of testing.

Test Bias — New Barriers for Minorities

As Dr. Howard Taylor of Rutgers University points out in *The IQ GAME*, standardized tests which are normed on predominantly white populations "depend heavily upon linguistic styles, which differ considerably between black and white populations in the United States, even with a control for socioeconomic status.[14]

Another indicator of test bias which is acknowleged to have an effect on minority students is their inability to identify with the characterizations in many test questions. Consider this item from the Lorge-Thorndike IQ test.

Which of the following words best completes this sentence:

"How the _____ roses flush up in the cheeks."

    (A) White
    (B) Pretty
    (C) Small
    (D) Yellow
    (E) Red

The answer, according to the testmakers who devised this question twenty years ago, is "red." But, of course, red is right only if the cheek in question is white. (See Exhibit 3).

Testing for the Public, a non-profit organization which trains minority students to take standardized tests, recently examined the Law School Admissions Test (LSAT) using information made public through New York's Truth-in-Testing law. Their research identified many items which contained derogatory references to prominent minority figures such as W.E.B. DuBois, Cesar Chavez and Harriet Tubman. They also found many items which could

---

[13]Madaus, 'Test Scores as Administrative Mechanisms in Educational Policy', *Phi Delta Kappan*, May 1985.
[14]Howard F. Taylor, *The I.Q. Game*, Rutgers University Press, 1980, p. 131.

be offensive to minority test takers. For example, the following recently administered LSAT items were supposed to measure a student's knowledge of grammar[15]:

>   *Afrikaans is the language **(A)of the ruling party in** South Africa and **(B)of** the Afrikaaners, **(C)whose vote (D)maintain** the status quo. **(E)No error**

>   *The Supreme Court ruled that it is not inherently unconstitutional for a white suburb to refuse to change zoning rules **which practical effect was to block** construction of racially integrated housing.

>   (A) which practical effect was to block
>   (B) which practical effect were to block
>   (C) which practical effect was to block
>   (D) of which the practical effects were blocking
>   (E) whose practical effects were blocked by

Students usually have less than a minute to answer each item on college and professional school multiple-choice exams. Testing for the Public's Executive Director, David White, points out that items such as those above may cause minority students to get angry or waste time thinking about the content of such questions. Accordingly, Mr. White trains minority students "to think white" and to read questions superficially when taking the exams.[16]

A 1980 study by Joseph Gannon for the National Conference of Black Lawyers provides further evidence of bias in the LSAT.[17] The large gap between the median LSAT scores of Blacks and whites has historically been rationalized by test publishers as the result of unequal educational opportunity.

Gannon's study took care to eliminate the possibility of lower academic ability on the part of minority students as an explanation for his findings. He examined the difference in LSAT scores of Black and white college seniors who had majored in the same departments of the same universities and earned comparable undergraduate grade point averages. As the following summary of Gannon's findings shows, even Blacks with comparable credentials to whites scored nearly 100 points lower on the LSAT.

---

[15]*Testing Digest*, spring 1980, p.12.
[16]Personal communication from Mr. White to the author, Fall 1986.
[17]Joseph Gannon, 'Future of Affirmative Action in Law School Admissions', National Conference of Black Lawyers, 1980.

Exhibit 4

GANNON LSAT CHART

Difference in LSAT Scores Between Whites & Minority Law Applicants Who Have Comparable Grades, Majors, & Undergraduate Institutions			
Minority Group	Number in Sample	Score Differences	
		Mean	Median
Blacks	722	-109.6	-101.1
Chicanos	352	- 99.4	-106.5
Native Amer.	48	- 77.8	- 79.9
Asian Amer.	277	- 34.5	- 23.8

There is ample data indicating that the cultural content of a question can alter students' scores.[18] Questions from recent SATs require students to be familiar with such activities as polo, golfing, tennis, minuets, pirouettes, property taxes, violins, melodeons and horseback riding. (See Exhibit 5) Students without this culturally-specific knowledge cannot obtain the high SAT scores needed to enter America's selective colleges or to become eligible for financial aid awards from private foundations and government agencies.

Recent lawsuits clearly illustrate how the gains made by minority workers can potentially be lost through the use of biased and discriminatory exams. In *Griggs v. Duke Power Company* of 1971 the Supreme Court ruled that any test is illegal unless it clearly measures skills needed for the job. Citing **Griggs** as a precedent courts have ordered that non-job related questions be removed from tests. For example, "What does R.S.V.P. signify?" was recently removed from Washington D.C.'s police promotion test following a suit brought by the Lawyers' Committee for Civil rights Under Law which claimed the test asked non job-related questions which unfairly discriminated against Blacks.[19]

---

[18]For example, see Donald Medley and Thomas Quirk, 'The Application of a Factorial Design to the Study of Cultural Bias in General Cultural Items on the National Teacher Examination', *Journal of Educational Measurement*, Winter 1974.

[19]See Lawyers' Committee for Civil Rights under Law, *Annual Report*, 1985-86, p. 3. (This Annual Report can be obtained from 1400 Eye Street, N.W., Suite 400, Washington, D.C. 20005).

Standardized Tests — Poor Indicators of Minority Performance

The problems caused by disparate scores and test bias are magnified by overreliance on standardized tests for evaluation, promotion, admission and licensing. Tests have been oversold and overused to the detriment of other, often better, predictors of performance. Many studies, including one conducted in 1985 by Dr. Peter Garcia, Dean of Education at Pan American University in Texas for the National Institute of Education, conclude that teacher licensing tests have no predictive ability for future performance.[20] ETS' own research reveals that SAT scores improve colleges' ability to predict first year college grades only marginally over what could be predicted using a student's high school grades — .52 for grades alone, .58 for grades and SAT scores.[21]

Charles Willie of Harvard's Graduate School of Education reports that at Ivy League colleges there is no correlation between admission test scores and academic performance during the fourth year for minority students, many of whom must make significant adjustments to the college environment.[22]

Professor Willie also found that "when (graduate school) admissions committees ignore applicants' scores on standardized tests, these committees tend to admit a higher proportion of minority students than they do when test scores are made a part of admissions decisions.[23]

"At the undergraduate level," Willie continued, "evidence also exists that the use of scores on standardized aptitude tests as part of the admissions process disproportionately excludes some racial and ethnic minorities. When, in 1977, the University of California proposed a change in its admissions policy that gave greater weight to standardized test scores than to high school grade-point averages, a member of the Board of Regents requested that the new criterion be applied hypothetically to the class that had been admitted the year before the new policy was proposed, in order to assess the potential effects of the change. The study revealed that, if the proposed admissions criterion had been in effect a year earlier, the total University of California student body would have included 9.5 percent fewer Hispanic students and 8.8 percent fewer black students...."[24]

[20]See Peter A. Garcia, 'A Study on Teacher Competency Testing and Test Validity with Implications for Minorities', National Institute of Education, 1985.
[21]Gerald W. Bracey, 'ETS as Big Brother: An Essay-Review', *Phi Delta Kappan*, September 1985, p. 77.
[22]Charles V. Willie, 'The Problem of Standardized Testing in a Free and Pluralistic Society', *Phi Delta Kappan*, May 1985.
[23]*Ibid.*
[24]*Ibid.*
[25]See *Education Week*, April 12, 1986.

Coaching — A Case of Double Jeopardy

As the use of tests has increased, a parallel phenomenon has developed — coaching for the tests. The SAT alone has spawned a thriving, multimillion dollar industry preparing students to take the test.

The coaching business ranges from private tutors (one Greenwich, Connecticut, school superintendent reports prices ranging to $60 per hour) to the coaching schools like Stanley H. Kaplan Education Centers and the Princeton Review (with tuition in the $400 - $600 range).

Both Kaplan and the Princeton Review claim average SAT score improvements in the 150-200 point range, an increase which can mean the difference between a rejection notice and college admission with a scholarship. This coaching boom puts minorities and low-income students in double jeopardy. Not only are they unable to afford the advantages promised by coaching, but the success of coaching increases the disparity between racial groups even further.

Educational Implications of Testing

As the use of standardized tests increases, their impact on the curriculum can be likened to that of the tail wagging the dog. Instead of using exams as aids in the educational process, schools are influenced to shape their curriculum to insure that teachers teach to the test. The study of literature and the practice of writing in English classes, for example, give way to memorizing analogies and multiple-choice vocabulary quizzes.[25]

Sometimes "teaching to the test" is the result of informal pressure to boost scores. Other times, it is the result of administrative directives. For example, St. Louis' Superintendent of Schools announced in 1985 that 60 teachers and principals would be fired because their students did not post sufficient gains on standardized multiple choice tests.[25]

The "wall chart" mentality fostered by U.S. Education Secretary William Bennett — whereby states are rank ordered by their students' performance on standardized tests — has further fueled this move toward test-driven instruction. Officials in Indiana and Georgia have even gone so far as to take steps to discourage low-scoring students from taking the SAT to boost their states' average scores — which they believe will improve their states' "business climate" ratings.[27]

---

[26]See *FairTest News Update*, no. 4, p. 4.
[27]See B. Powell and L.C. Steelman, 'Variations in State SAT Performance: Meaningful or Misleading', *Harvard Education Review*, November, 1984.

The Unaccountable Testing Industry

Public policy protects the food we eat, the products we buy, the safety standards at our workplaces. Yet, despite its overwhelming impact on both citizens and institutions, the testing industry is essentially unregulated. Few consumer protection laws apply, and test publishers refuse to voluntarily provide elected government officials, independent researchers and test takers themselves with information needed to verify that their exams are fair and valid.

Both individuals who believe they have been wronged by a standardized test and the growing testing reform movement in this country have been seriously hampered by the inaccessibility of information. Without access to data they cannot investigate abuses or design remedial procedures. In March, 1977, the late Dr. Oscar Buros, editor of the authoritative *Mental Measurements Yearbook*, lamented, "Today it is practically impossible for a competent test technician or test consumer to make a thorough appraisal of the construction, validation, and use of standardized tests...because of the limited amount of trustworthy information supplied by test publishers."[28]

Even federal government sources of information on tests are controlled by test publishers. For example, America's largest testing firm, Educational Testing Service, operates the Federal government's Education Research Information Center on Tests, Measurement and Evaluation, the nation's "official" clearinghouse distributing information on standardized tests and other methods of evaluating students and workers.

Steps Toward Reform

Mounting evidence documents that standardized multiple-choice exams often provide little indication of a person's ability and unfairly discriminate against Blacks, Hispanics, rural Americans, females, and unusually creative people of all backgrounds. Despite these serious flaws, it is not likely that the number of standardized tests administered each year will decline in the near future. Until new forms of evaluation are developed, simplistic numerical scores from these exams will continue to influence the educational and employment opportunities of millions of Americans.

In the short run, five simple safeguards can dramatically improve the quality and fairness of these influential tests.

First, Truth-in-Testing provisions should be extended to all standardized tests used by schools, universities and occupational licensing agencies.

---

[28]Quoted in Andrew J. Strenio, Jr., *The Testing Trap*, Rawson, Wade, Publisher, Inc., 1981, . 274.

Much of the evidence about the flaws in college and graduate school admissions tests cited above was disclosed under Truth-in-Testing provisions adopted in California and New York in the late 1970s.[29] These laws forced test publishers to make public — for the first time — old copies of exams, as well as studies concerning their tests' accuracy, validity and cultural biases.

In addition Truth-in-Testing requires exam makers to publicly defend or re-score items which test-takers challenge as inaccurate or biased. Over a million students' scores have already been raised due to errors discovered through Truth-in-Testing laws.

Unfortunately, the California and New York laws cover less than 15% of the standardized exams administered each year. Everyone taking a standardized test should have the ability to review copies of the scored exams which will determine their educational or career opportunities. In addition, independent researchers must have the data needed to examine test makers' claims that their exams are valid and not unfairly biased against any economic or racial group.

Next, the "Golden Rule" principle should be applied to all standardized exams. This simple statistical technique requires replacement of discriminatory questions with less biased items of equal difficulty testing the same subject area. It is based on a November 1984 out-of-court agreement between the Educational Testing Service, the State of Illinois, and the Golden Rule Insurance Company of Illinois. ETS agreed to employ this new procedure to settle a lawsuit charging that their Illinois Insurance Agent Licensing Exam was not job-related and unfairly discriminated against Blacks. A November, 1986, judicial ruling extended a similar reform to teacher tests in Alabama.[30] Legislators in California, Massachusetts, New York, Rhode Island, Texas and Wisconsin are currently considering whether to extend the Golden Rule reforms to exams administered in their states.[31]

The Golden Rule principle helps ensure that tests measure relevant knowledge differences among test-takers and not irrelevant, culturally-specific information. Under the procedure, the same content areas will be covered as on previous tests and the exams will be of the same level of overall difficulty. The only difference is that within groups of equally

[29]See Legislative Report on Truth-in-Testing, published by Senator Kenneth LaValle, Chair of the New York State Higher Education Committee, Albany, NY 12247.
[30]For details of the Allen v. Alamaba State Board of Education ruling, which challenged the constitutionality of a state teacher-testing program that had a disproportionate minority failure rate, see *Education Week*, December 10, 1986.
[31]For information on current Golden Rule initiatives, see FairTest News Update, no. 4, or contact: FairTest, P.O. Box 1272, Harvard Square Station, Cambridge, MA 02238.

difficult items in the same content areas, test publishers must select those items that display the least difference in the correct answer rates between majority and minority test-takers. Thus, the Golden Rule bias reduction safeguard makes exams *fairer, not easier.* As Emory University Psychology Professor Martin Shapiro told *The New York Times*, "Once you have this method, to not use it is to knowingly use a more discriminatory procedure."[32]

To understand why the Golden Rule reform is needed, one needs to examine how most test publishers currently construct their exams. For example, on the SAT, ETS develops a large pool of potential questions for each content level. After pretesting these items on a sample group of test-takers, ETS discards those items which it believes are ambiguous, biased or otherwise flawed. From the remaining pool of items, ETS employs a statistical technique — based on r-biserial correlations — that selects for the final SAT those pre-tested questions that *maximize* the difference between high and low-scoring test takers.

Often questions which *maximize* differences between high and low scoring students really are measuring a test-taker's knowledge of some culturally-specific information. For example, examine the following SAT item:[33]

RUNNER:MARATHON

    (A) envoy:embassy
    (B) martyr:massacre
    (C) oarsman:regatta
    (D) referee:tournament
    (E) horse:stable

53% of the whites, but just 22% of the blacks gave the wanted answer, (c). 20% of the students would have obtained the correct answer if they had just guessed. Clearly this item does not measure students' "aptitude" or logical reasoning ability, but knowledge of upper middle-class recreational activity. The Golden Rule reform would replace this item with another analogy question that did not require esoteric, culturally-specific knowledge.

Third, test publishers must take responsibility for how their tests are actually used. Standardized tests are like drugs — properly used they can sometimes be beneficial — but if misused they can cause enormous damage. A test designed for one purpose or group can have disastrous consequences if it is administered to a different group or used for an unvalidated purpose.

---

[32]*The New York Times*, November 29, 1984.
[33]Cited in Thomas F. Donlon, 'The SAT in a Diverse Society: Fairness and Sensitivity', *College Board News*, Winter 1981-2, p. 20.

Instead of simply issuing pronouncements about inappropriate test use, testing companies must take affirmative action to stop misuses and abuses. Unless they voluntarily make reforms, civil rights and educational groups should seek judicial and legislative action to force them to act responsibly.

Fourth, organizations that require tests should conduct independent studies to determine if the tests they require are really valid. Often universities and government agencies rely on studies conducted by test publishers to evaluate their need for an exam. This is like asking General Motors to conduct a study to determine what brand of car you should purchase. Within the last two years, based on their own independent research, Bates College stopped requiring the SAT, Harvard Business School the GMAT, and Johns Hopkins Medical School the MCAT.

Finally, there must be an independent information source for researchers, test-takers, policy makers and the public about the accuracy and cultural biases of these exams. While the federal government theoretically has just such an entity — the Educational Resource Information Center on Tests, Measurement and Evaluation (ERIC/TME) — it is operated by America's largest testing company, the Educational Testing Service.

Having ETS operate this ERIC/TME Clearinghouse is like having a fox guard the chicken coop. FairTest has documented that ETS uses its control of ERIC/TME to unfairly promote company products and philosophy[36].

---

[34]The Larry P. v. Wilson Riles case could serve as a legal precedent not only in California, but throughout the jurisdiction of the U.S. Court of Appeals for the Ninth Circuit (Arizona, Idaho, Montana, Nevada, Oregon and Washington). See *Education Week*, November 12, 1986.
[35]See *FairTest News Update*, nos. 1, 3, 4.
[36]See the *Chronicle of Higher Education*, September 10, 1986 and *Education Week*, November 19, 1986.

Exhibit 5

SAMPLE QUESTIONS FROM RECENT
SCHOLASTIC APTITUDE TESTS
(cite)

(1) RACQUET:TENNIS::
   (A) springboard:diver
   (B) horse:polo
   (C) glove:boxing
   (C) club:golf *
   (E) gun:hunting

(2) HEIRLOOM:INHERITANCE::
   (A) payment:currency
   (B) belongings:receipt
   (C) land:construction
   (D) legacy:bill
   (E) booty:plunder *

(3) CONSERVATORY:MUSIC::
   (A) anthology:books
   (B) aerie:birds
   (C) bivouac:army
   (D) seminary:religion *
   (E) arbor:grapes

(4) SONATA:MUSIC::
   (A) epic:whimsical
   (B) novel:literary *
   (C) song:humorous
   (D) testimony:rhymed
   (E) pantomime:vocal

(5) MINUET:DANCE::
   (A) beret:bowler
   (B) clarinet:symphony
   (C) chariot:wheel
   (D) sonnet:poem *
   (E) gown:petticoat

(6) PIROUETTE:DANCE::
   (A) touchdown:referee
   (B) motivation:coach
   (C) somersault:acrobat *
   (D) model:sculptor
   (E) rink:skater

(7) MELODEON:ORGANIST::
   (A) reveille:bugler
   (B) solo:accompanist
   (C) crescendo:pianist
   (D) anthem:choirmaster
   (E) kettledrum:tympanist *

(8) BRIDLE:HORSE::
   (A) bone:dog
   (B) olive branch:dove
   (C) valor:soldier
   (D) precept:conduct *
   (E) devotion:duty

(* — wanted answer)

Every few years the U.S. Dept. of Education puts the contract to run this clearinghouse out for competitive bid. ETS always submits below-cost bids because company executives realize the advantages of controlling access to information about their products.[37] Secretary of Education Bennett should rule that it is improper for a company that annually earns nearly $200 million from selling tests to control the government's official clearinghouse about the products they sell.

Conclusion

America needs tests and other forms of evaluation. But we need not accept at face value the testing industry's claim that all their exams are fair and accurate. Instead, we need tools like Truth-in-Testing and Golden Rule to examine the examiners. Tests that prove to be culturally-biased or invalid must be overhauled or discarded.

John Weiss helped Congressman Michael Harrington (D-MA) draft the first federal Truth-in-Testing Legislation in 1977. Currently he is the Executive Director of the National Center for Fair & Open Testing (FairTest) P.O. Box 1272, Harvard Square Station, Cambridge, MA 02238 (617) 864-4810.

---

[37]*Ibid.*

College Admissions & Coaching
by
Beverly P. Cole

The use of college entrance exams as the primary criterion for admission to institutions of higher education has created controversy for the past 30 years. Critics of these exams have been quite vocal in the black community where black students have routinely scored approximately one standard deviation below their white counterparts.

The two major exams used in the admissions process is the Scholastic Aptitude Test (SAT) produced by The Educational Testing Service (ETS), and The American College Testing Program (ACT).

The SAT which consists of two parts (math and verbal) is scored from 200-800 on each part. The mathematical section includes computation and the application of the principles of arithmetic, algebra, and geometry. The verbal section is based on vocabulary, verbal reasoning, relationships, and reading comprehension.

The ACT tests which assess the areas of english, mathematics, social studies, and natural science are more closely aligned with the academic curricula than the SAT and its composite score ranges from 1-36.

Do the Entrance Exams Play An Important Role In the Admission Process?

Although 2.5 million students took these tests for admissions purposes (the majority taking the SAT), there is a raging debate as to the actual significance placed on the test score by the various post-secondary institutions.

Ernest Boyer, the President of The Carnegie Foundation for the Advancement of Teaching, feels that the tests should be abandoned since only a few of the very selective colleges are placing significant weight on the scores for admission, while others are just requiring the tests.

In an indepth study of 29 colleges and universities, and independent surveys of 5,000 college students, and 5,000 faculty members, the question was asked of the admission directors, "How would have last year's freshman class differed without the use of the SAT's or ACT's? Sixty-two percent of the respondents replied that it would have made little or no difference."[1]

James Crouse in the *Harvard Educational Review*, argues that most admission officers select their applicants based on a composite of variables such as the SAT score and high school class rank. Crouse maintains that if either variable is used, identical admission decisions would be made on 90.8 percent of the applicants. Only 9.2 percent would be accepted using one variable but not the other, regardless of where the cutoff point is set. He, thereby, concludes that the costs of the SAT in terms of the time and money expended being coached, as well as, the anxiety created, is not worth the

---

[1]*New York Times*, "Debating Use of SAT Tests," November 11, 1986.

retention of the requirement, when one knows that the high school rank policy compared to a high school rank, plus SAT policy makes no difference in the selection of most applicants.[2]

Hartnett and Feldmesser also maintain that most institutions are none selective but require the test scores only to maintain their aura of selectivity.[3] This aura of selectivity is reinforced by educators and the media. The best colleges are the choosiest colleges, i.e., those that select the highest scoring students. A recent article in the *U.S.A. Today* newspaper ran the headline, "What Are the Choosiest Colleges in the Country?" the subheading was 'Taking The Cream Of the Crop.' "Here are the 46 U.S.A. universities that accepted less than half of the applicants last year and had an average freshman SAT score of 1,200 or more out of 1,600."[4] This type of policy which is very elitist in nature, sanctions the wholesale elimination of large numbers of students whom it finds unworthy to educate. Since students are encouraged to use their scores to help them make decisions about college choices, the screening out process begins at a much earlier stage.

Boyer, in his report - *College: The Undergraduate Experience In America*, maintains that this scare effect seriously affects minority students. This year, the Educational Testing Service reported a 5 percent decline in the number of black students taking the SAT. In addition, 62 percent of the students interviewed in the Boyer study, felt that their scores would rule out the college they would most like to attend.[5] If indeed, the entrance exams are not a crucial component of the admission process, then a cruel hoax is being perpetuated on our youth.

Contrary to the above stated opinions, are several studies which attest to the fact that the SAT and the ACT are alive, well, flourishing, and significant.

One of the older, but more thorough studies was done by Wing and Wallach (1971). After a careful analysis of data from 224 colleges with varying degrees of selectivity, they found that the tests were extremely important in admissions decisions. "Relatively small differences were found to alter the applicants' chances significantly.[6]

---

[2]James Crouse, "Does the SAT help Colleges Make Better Selection Decisions?" *Harvard Educational Review*, Vol. 55, No. 2, May, 1985, pp. 202-217.

[3]Rodney T. Hartnett and Robert A. Feldmesser, "College Admissions Testing and the Myth of Selectivity," AAHE Bulletin, 32 (March, 1980).

[4]*U.S.A. Today*, "What Are the Choosiest Colleges In the Country?", December 15, 1986.

[5]*Op. cit.*, New York Times, Nov. 11, 1986.

[6]Cliff W. Wing, Jr. and Michael A. Wallach "College Admissions and the Psychology of Talent (New York: Holt, Rinehart & Winston 1971) pp. 39, 41, 56.

Although the margin of error for the SAT is approximately 30 (plus or minus) points, Wing and Wallach found that score difference of 60 points could alter the chances for selection by more than 100%.[7]

Of the 2,000-plus colleges listed in the *Peterson's Guide To Colleges*, 68 percent require applicants to take the SAT or the ACT.[8] In addition, the American College Testing Program reported that approximately 90 percent of the 1,700 four-year undergraduate schools in the United States currently require either the SAT or ACT.[9]

A recent survey conducted by the National Association of Secondary School Principals sought to determine the degree of increase in admission requirements. The major four-year public institution or system in each state was contacted. Eighteen indicated the minimum ACT or SAT score requirements for admission, which ranged from 15-27 for the ACT and 720 to 1,150 for the SAT. Three state institutions indicated a weighted combination of SAT or ACT and high school percentile rank, class rank, or grade point average.[10]

The most comprehensive study sponsored by the College Board and the American Association of Collegiate Registrars and Admissions Officers (AACRAO) compiled the responses of 1,463 institutions. Included in this tabulation are 63.1 percent of the public four-year institutions and 56.8 percent of the private institutions.

The College Board/AACRAO data reveal that 63 percent of the public four-year colleges and 55 percent of the private four-year colleges consider the entrance examinations to be the single most important factor or a very important factor in admission decisions. Sixty-one percent of the public four-year colleges and 65% of the private four-year colleges require the SAT or ACT of all their applicants.

When asked if there were minimum SAT or ACT scores beyond which an applicant is generally not considered for admission, approximately 38 percent of public four-year colleges and 42 percent of private four-year colleges answered yes for the SAT, while 20 percent of the public and 36 percent of the private answered yes for the ACT. The SAT minimum for the public was 740 and 754 for the private. For the ACT composites, the average was 16.2 for the public and 16.4 for the private. According to the respond-

---

[7]*Ibid.*

[8]Allan Narin, et. al., The Reign of ETS (Washington, D.C. Ralph Nader, 1980), p. 48.

[9]Rodney Skayer, "On The Use and Importance of Tests of *Ability In Admission To Post-Secondary Education,*" in *Ability Testing: Uses, Consequences, and Controversies* II (Washington, D.C. - National Academy Press, 1982), pp. 289-290.

[10]National Association of Secondary School Principals. College Admissions: New Requirement By the State Universities (Reston, Va., 1983).

ing institutions, this pattern of importance given to tests will remain unchanged throughout the 80's.[11] It must be remembered that this study was conducted in 1980 before the reform movement in Education started. Now with the increased emphasis on excellence and the test score as evidence of its attainment, this projection might be increased if made today.

Are The Entrance Exams Valid Predictors Of College Success?

Several colleges have questioned the validity of the entrance exams as instruments for selection. After a two-year study, Bowdoin College discovered that only 31% of all honors graduates had scored above the class average on both the SAT's, while 24 percent had scored below. Although Bowdoin discontinued the SAT requirement in 1979, it is still considered one of the more selective institutions.[12]

Williams College conducted a 10-year experiment of admitting 10% of each year's class, who would otherwise have been rejected due to their scores. The identities of the students were kept confidential and they were subjected to the same academic curricula as the other students without any special aid. The findings of the study revealed that 72 percent of the students had graduated compared to Williams' average of 85 percent; in one graduating class, the class president, president of the college council, and president of the honor society, had all been admitted under the special program. Because of those findings, that policy is continued today.[13]

ETS has always claimed that the SAT predicts freshman grade point average. The median correlation of SAT - verbal with freshman GPA is .38, and the median for the SAT - math is .34. Because of the relationship between the size of a correlation coefficient and the accuracy of prediction, it can safely be concluded that people with the same SAT scores will have wide variability in their GPA's. The median correlation of the combination of four ACT scores with freshman GPA has been close to .50.

Neither the SAT or ACT have been found to be a better or even as good predictor of freshman GPA, as high school grades or high school rank in class. The addition of test scores to high school grades increase the correlation by .05 to .10 for the SAT and ACT.

Linn maintains that ACT and SAT scores are related to freshman GPA for both whites and blacks, but the relationship tends to be somewhat higher for whites than blacks. When high school grades are combined with test

---

[11]The College Board and The American Association of Collegiate Registrars and Admissions Officers, *Undergraduate Admissions: The Realities of Institutional Policies, Practices and Procedures* (New York: College Entrance Examination board, 1980), pp. 10, 17, 24, 28.

[12]David Owen, *None of the Above* (Boston: Houghton Mifflin, 1985), p. 241.

[13]Allan Narin, *the Reign of ETS* (Washington, D.C.: Ralph Nader, 1980) p. 74.

scores, the tendency for freshman GPA to be predicted somewhat better for whites than for blacks is still observed.[14]

Williams cites a study conducted by Davis and Temp which concluded that there is no evidence of bias against blacks on the basis of difference in the SAT and grades. Blacks who make a given score on the SAT do not achieve different GPA's than their white counterparts. Williams, however, reports that of the 19 institutions evaluated, in the same study, the SAT predicted grades for white students in 18 of the 19 institutions, or in 95% of the cases.[15]

It should be stressed that the entrance examinations do not claim to predict college success, just the first year GPA. However, at many institutions, they continue to be treated as if they are the absolute measure of intellectual worth.

It has been found that the predictive validity of the admission tests and high school grades decline from one semester to the next during the college years. The correlation of the ACT composite scores with eighth semester GPA at one university was only .17. The first semester GPA correlation with the eighth semester GPA was only .34, which represented a steady decline and an instability in academic performance.[16]

Alexander Astin conducted an analysis of factors that influence minority students' educational development. He reviewed approximately 30 outcome measures such as college grade-point average, undergraduate persistence, satisfaction with the undergraduate college, attainment of a baccalaureate degree, etc. His conclusion was that the students' academic aptitude as measured by standard admissions tests (SAT and the ACT) did not show substantial relationships to many outcomes.[17]

It was Astin's feelings that the student's ability to stay in college was a more appropriate measure of his success than his freshman grades.

In spite of the fact that serious questions have been raised against the admissions exams regarding their validity, the tests continue to be used to the detriment of minorities and the poor.

---

[14]Robert Linn, "Ability Testing: Individual Differences, Predication, and Differential Prediction in *Ability Testing: Uses, Consequences, and Controversies II* (Washington, D.C.: National Academy Press, 1982) p. 343.

[15]Robert L. Williams, "The Black Student In Higher Education: The Zero Sum Game," Paper presented at the National Education Conference, Washburn University, Topeka, Kansas.

[16]Op. cit. Linn, "Ability Testing: Individual Differences, Prediction & Differential Prediction," pp. 349-352.

[17]Alexander Astin, Minorities In American Higher Education (San Francisco: Jossey-Bass Publishers, 1982) p. 92.

Doermann reports that the score/income correlation is higher than the correlation found between the SAT and first year GPA. He further states that the coefficient of correlation for the black students is even higher.[18]

Is Coaching For the Entrance Exams Effective?

As institutions of higher education continue to require the admissions test, as well as, raise the cut-off scores, it becomes incumbent upon all concerned with enrollment in higher education to assist the prospective student by preparing him/her to take the SAT or ACT - a practice which is known as "coaching."

For many years, ETS has claimed that its aptitude tests were impervious to short-term improvements by cramming or coaching. Nevertheless, commercial coaching schools have made millions of dollars by charging from $400 + for six-week courses that do just that.

The wealthy have been able to take advantage of this option which has rarely been available to the poor. Suburban school districts and private schools have provided these review courses while the urban and rural schools which are often hard-pressed for funds, cannot afford to do so. In a 1979 comparison of coached and uncoached students, 41.2 percent of the students coached came from families with incomes in excess of $30,000.[19] This is certainly one factor that could explain the great variance in test scores. But is coaching effective?

The Federal Trade Commission in its 1979 report concluded that despite denials by ETS and the College Board, coaching can be effective and a determinant factor in deciding who is admitted to colleges and universities. One re-analysis found that after background factors were taken into account, the score gains to be expected due to coaching on the SAT were 25 points on both the Math and Verbal Section.[20] Evidence presented by Warner Slack and Douglas Porter indicates that training for the Scholastic Aptitude Test can effectively help students raise their scores. Their analyses of studies revealed an average gain of 29 points for the SAT-V and 33 points for the SAT-M.[21]

---

[18]Humphrey Doerman, *Crosscurrents In College Admissions* (New York: Columbia Teachers College Press 1970) pp. 147-49.

[19]Federal Trade Commission, Bureau of Consumer Protection, *Effects of Coaching On Standardized Admission Examinations*: Revised Statistical Analyses of Data Gathered By - Boston Regional Office of The Federal Trade Commission, March 1979) p. 8.

[20]*Ibid.*

[21]Warner V. Slack and Douglas Porter, "The Scholastic Aptitude Test: A Critical Appraisal," *Harvard Educational Review* (Vol. 50, No. 2, 1980).

After a detailed review of coaching studies, Nancy Cole concluded that the bulk of evidence indicated that coaching can often produce detectable differences in students' scores. She further stated that the size of the coaching effects, usually around 10-25 points, appears significant enough to some students and some colleges to make it worthwhile for students in highly competitive admissions situations to seek coaching.[22]

Messick's review and re-analysis of research from the 1950's to the present concluded that "overall the smaller coaching effects appear to be associated with short-term, relatively non-intensive practice and review, and the larger effects (which occur more for math than for verbal) appear to be associated with longer term, high student contact programs focusing on skill development."[23] Messick believes that students who are willing to invest 20 hours or so can be expected to increase their verbal score by 12 to 13 points and about 20 points on the mathematical section. After that, the law of diminishing returns sets in. A 30-point average gain on the SAT-V comes after about 300 hours of coaching.

Messick, however, has acknowledged that certain types of students, including some members of minority groups, may be able to increase their scores much more than the average through commercial or other test preparation courses.[24]

This statement refers to the most significant research finding yet to support coaching for blacks, the Stroud "Re-Analysis of the FTC Study of Commercial Coaching For the SAT." According to Stroud's analysis, race and parental income were the most significant predictor variables contributing to the verbal individual coaching effect. Of the 13 black students identified at one coaching school, the average verbal coaching effect was 46.7 points above that for white students, which was significant at the .001 level. Stroud stated that even though the sample consisted of only 13 students, the size of the effect was quite large and highly significant statistically. The average math effect for the black students also exceeded that for the whites, but the difference was not statistically significant. Verbal effects were found for the black students at the other coaching school,

---

[22]Nancy Cole, "The Implications of Coaching For Ability Testing," in *Ability Testing: Uses, Consequences, and Controversies II* (Washington, D.C.: National Academy Press, 1982) p. 406.

[23]Samuel Messick, The Effectiveness of Coaching For The SAT: Review and Re-analysis of Research From the Fifties to the FTC. (Princeton, N.J.: Educational Testing Service, 1980) p. 29.

[24]Samuel Messick, "Coaching On SAT's May Mean Up To 20 Points," *New York Times*, December 23, 1980, p. C1.

103

which exceeded the mean by 24.6 points on the average. Six additional black students were identified who had taken the SAT, their verbal effects exceeded their corresponding cell means by 52.6 points on the average.

Whatever the basis for this black phenomenon, it did not transfer to minorities, in general. When data for non-black minority students were examined, their coaching effects bore more resemblance to those of white students than black students. It should also be noted that the second most important predictor variable in the multiple regression equation was self-reported parental income.[25]

The only possible explanation for this phenomenon is that blacks and the poor have an initial disadvantage in test-taking that can be overcome by coaching. For many students, the SAT may be more a reflection of their social class or race than of their potential for accomplishment.

Test Preparation Clinics

The NAACP has historically fought to remove, for its constituents, the barriers to upward mobility and obstacles that hinder entrance into the American mainstream. Therefore, it was only natural for it to get involved with and challenge the admission tests which deny access to high education for many minority youth.

In 1976, in an effort to express its concern, the National NAACP convened a Conference On Minority Testing which brought together educators, test producers, and civil rights leaders. They agreed on a number of recommendations that would provide for greater public understanding of the misuses and limits of these tests, as well as, ways to remove the cultural bias. Their suggestions are contained in the publication, *NAACP Report On Minority Testing*.

Based on the recommendations of that report and the findings of the Stroud analysis, the NAACP appointed an advisory group of psychometricians to design test preparation workshops for low-income black students since their scores were by far the lowest on the SAT.

Pilot workshops were set-up in three cities: New York, San Francisco, and Atlanta. The test preparation clinics consisted of a total of 14 sessions held bi-weekly for 2½ to three hours. The sessions ended just prior to the actual SAT testing session. Two clinics were held in each city serving a total of 215 students.

---

[25]*Ibid*. "Estimation Of Combined Coaching/Self-Selection Effects In the FTC Study: Detailed Summary and Elaboration Of the Stroud Re-Analysis," pp. 49, 50, 48.

The format of each clinic consisted of:

I. **Student-Parent Orientation**

This session was held prior to the actual workshops. Students were registered for the clinic by their parents. A discussion was held concerning the importance of the exam and the logistics of the workshops. Parents were requested to sign a pledge promising to encourage student attendance and the completion of homework assignments.

II. **Administration of Pretest and Post-Test**

The instruments used, called the SAT Prep, were developed from actual SAT tests which had been released by ETS. Four parallel forms, labelled A, B, C, and D were developed by halving two existing tests. This was comparable to the PSAT. The use of parallel forms meant that all participants would have a different form for the pretest and post-test. (The Test For Standard Written English was omitted). Each form of the SAT-Prep took one hour to administer. These tests were developed by Dr. Sylvia Johnson of Howard University Using standard equating procedures, SAT-type scores on a 200-800 scale were estimated from the half length tests. Permission was obtained from ETS for the use of the items.

III. **Introduction and Overview**

The **politics of testing** was discussed with the youth. Such issues as testing as a barrier to access, the validity of entrance examinations in predicting college success; the effectiveness of coaching, the myth about "aptitude," and counseling for higher education, in general, which most of these inner city students had not had, were discussed.

Test-wiseness strategies were taught such as, time use, understanding and following directions, guessing effectively, answer elimination strategies, becoming familiar with the type of questions asked and, the scoring system.

Assistance was also provided on how to deal with test anxiety.

IV. **Instructional Sessions**

The instructional sessions consisted of six math, six verbal, and one for the Test of Standard Written English.

Instructors, who were experienced high school teachers with strong academic and personal qualifications, attended a one-day training session in order to understand the program and its philosophy, and to assure conformity.

The findings of this study clearly support the effectiveness of a coaching program for improving the SAT-Prep performance of those black youth who had earned relatively low or mid-range scores on a pretest. Statistically, significant and important gains were found for participants in San Francisco and Atlanta, and for one session of the New York participants. These average gains ranged from 24 to 49 points on each of the two SAT tests.

After conducting an item analysis of all pretest and post-test questions, the most striking result was the finding that the students increased sharply the number of items reached on the post-test, compared to the pretest. Moving closer to the completion of the test was a result of many factors, pacing, better understanding of subject mater, familiarity with test directions and format, lower anxiety while working on the test, improved confidence, and a feeling of being better prepared.[26]

If the SAT truly measured aptitude, then one could not coach so effectively. The NAACP's two-month project did not make geniuses out of anyone. However, it did determine that a lot of low-income black students are not being counseled adequately concerning admission requirements. Many are walking in to testing centers with very little advance preparation. The College Board reports that the percentage of black students in an academic or college preparatory program is only 65 percent compared to 79 percent for all students; and that the average black student takes 1.14 fewer years of academic subjects.[27]

The over reliance on admissions tests by institutions of higher education is prematurely truncating the educational development of many intelligent youngsters, especially minorities. It has been shown that you can take these youngsters and raise their scores on the SAT. But what does this prove? Are they any smarter or more capable than they were before they took the coaching workshop?

A case in point, The University Institute of Technology has found a unique way of recruiting minority students. The students take a course to improve their college entrance test scores, and their chances of being accepted by the Institute of Technology. The University pays the students to take the coaching course. Before taking the coaching course, none of the 39 students had high enough SAT scores to allow them to be admitted to The

---

[26]Sylvia Johnson, "Preparing Black Students For the SAT — Does It Make A Difference?" (New York: NAACP, 1984)

[27]Leonard Ramist and Solomon Arbeiter, *Profiles, College-Bound Seniors, 1985* (New York: College Entrance Examination Board, 1986).

Institute of Technology. However, after the course, 13 of the students had made it pass the cut-off.[28]

It is obvious that we must institute a more rational approach for admission to higher education. Boyer argues this case when he concludes, "There is an urgent need for new and better ways to assess students as they move from school to higher education. The goal of the new assessment program would be to evaluate not only the academic achievement of students linking it to the curriculum that the students studied - but also to provide advisement, to help students make decisions more intelligently about their futures."[29]

Our society can ill-afford to be remiss in developing all potential.

---

[28]*Black Issues In Higher Education*, "University of Minnesota's Engineering Outreach Effort A Success - Unique Program Tackles SAT Problem," December 1, 1986 (Vol. 3, No. 16) p. 4.
[29]Ernest Boyer, "College: The Undergraduate Experience," in the *Chronicle of Higher Education*, November 5, 1986 (Vol. XXXIII, No. 10), p. 18.

BEYOND THE I.Q. FIASCO:

The Struggle for a Revolution in Professional Practice

The Ideology of Intelligence and I.Q. Magic in Education

by
Asa G. Hilliard, III

I don't see any point in I.Q. testing in schools. There's no more point in measuring I.Q. than in measuring the basal metabolic rate. Pupils, teachers, and parents need to know whether a pupil is learning what the school is trying to teach, but I can't see that they need to know the child's I.Q.[1]

I believe that the future will bring increasingly valid models of how the mind works in the learning process. It may also bring pedagogical applications for these valid models, applications which improve **teaching** and **learning**. It is even possible that the testing of mental dynamics may be accomplished by standardized procedures which can be performed cheaply, efficiently, and for the entrepreneur, even at a profit. That time is not now for the standardized I.Q. tests which are in widespread use in schools.

Let me be clear at the outset. I am looking primarily at the **utility** of both I.Q. tests and the construct intelligence for teaching practice. While the construct intelligence remains undefined operationally among the community of scholars, and while the tests to measure intelligent behavior cannot be shown to be universally valid instruments, these are technical matters for designers within the profession. During a research phase, wide latitude can be tolerated. However, when professional applications are made and where legal mandates for the use of instruments are involved, rigor in validity must be assured.

No position can be taken on whether "it" ("intelligence") is genetic or environmental until we have sufficient data to determine if "it" even exists; and if so, in what form. Similarly, it is premature to debate whether sorting by intelligence should be done by tests for school purposes unless the existence of intelligence can first be established and can be validly related to instruction. The test for utility must be made, determining if thinking with the construct of intelligence and/or testing with I.Q. tests makes a positive impact on the teaching-learning environment.

Finally, let me emphasize that I do support valid assessment. I also believe that psychology has much to offer teaching. At present, I.Q. test offering is only patent medicine.

The construct "intelligence" and the I.Q. tests which were designed to measure the behavior implied by the construct were fabricated and were

---

[1]Arthur Jensen, "Jensen Condemns Minimum Competency I.Q. Tests in the Schools," *Phi Delta Kappan*, vol. 61, no. 1, (1979), p. 75.

applied in education **prior** to the time that mental functions were even described clearly. Mental "measure" went from "research" through development to general application in an amazingly short time. Public school policy makers needed something like I.Q. tests; and presto! they were there.[2] "Intelligence" then, as now, was said by I.Q. test advocates to be **measured precisely**, before it could even be defined operationally in a common way by the community of scientists. There was not then, nor has there been since then, any general professional requirement that this undefined substance be measured in a uniform and rigorous way or that it be measured with instruments that yield comparable data. For example, the "subtests" on various I.Q. tests follow every conceivable pattern. Does each represent a component of intelligence? If not, then what is the meaning of a "subtest"? If so, does intelligence vary with the test?

Still, no matter how poor a construct, instrument, or procedure for mental measurement might appear to be, any serious educator could and would overlook the lack of construct and instrument refinement, **if the use of constructs, instruments, or procedures resulted in improved performance in teaching and learning.** Has this happened? I know of no data to show that it has. There are few professional researchers who seem willing to dare to ask the question.

It can be observed that the construct intelligence and the I.Q. tests which purport to measure the behavior implied by it are in almost universal use in the public schools. Among current popular uses for I.Q. tests are the following:

1. To determine a child's "**readiness**" for kindergarten.
2. to **predict** a person's future academic performance.
3. To **classify** a pupil for placement in special schools or programs.
4. To determine if a child is "**socially competent**."
5. To "**diagnose**" learning difficulties.

Yet we may ask again, is teaching and learning improved as a consequence of the use of I.Q. tests? The startling thing which one discovers when trying to answer that question, is that it is almost impossible even to establish criteria by which answers to the questions can be judged! It is really not clear just what is supposed to happen under ideal circumstances. Some of the reasons for this are simple. Professional language in testing is full of gross ambiguities. The full range of assumptions upon which professional discourse is based is seldom made explicit. Where implicit

---

[2]Murray Levine, "The Academic Achievement Test," *American Psychologist*, vol. 31 (1976), pp. 228-238.

assumptions can be inferred, they are hopelessly confounded. This confounding is evident as discussants in the intelligence and I.Q. debate slide back and forth from one set of assumptions to another, giving little evidence that they are aware that the shifts have been made. Let's take an example. I.Q. testing may be used for a variety of school purposes. They may be used for **sorting** and **classification**, for diagnosis of learning difficulties, for the development of **individual educational plans**, for **research** on thinking, and for **selection** for admission to education opportunities. Yet it is anything but clear just how a given I.Q. test such as a Wechsler or Binet can be used to serve all these diverse needs. If, for example, I.Q. test advocates are challenged to demonstrate "prescriptive" or pedagogical validity[3] for the test for a particular purpose, arguments which more logically support an entirely different purpose may be marshalled by test defenders. The arguments in support of the validation of a particular test as an individual **diagnostic device would hardly be expected to be the same as arguments in support of that same test as a program sorting** device.

Therefore, for example, the **diagnosis** of many African-American children by the use of a standardized I.Q. test may be challenged as invalid because such tests use an unfamiliar European-American vocabulary as a part of the "measure" of "mental capacity." This challenge is met frequently by a spurious argument. The spurious argument is that "all Americans should, for practical reasons, master the general culture." Notice that the challenge raised questions regarding the **valid measurement** of such things on I.Q. tests as remembering large numbers of words, using words "properly," etc. If different children are to be compared, these things should be "measured" **using a vocabulary which all tested children have had an equal opportunity to learn**. I.Q. test advocates' responses to the challenge above tend to change the focus of the discussion from points about the "**measurement**" of "**mental functions**" to a focus on the **practical utility** of a common language. Such a response about **utility** is true but irrelevant to the issue of measuring the child's dynamic patterns of thought.

There are other dimensions to the discussion which create similar confounding in discourse, for example, each time the **audience** for the information changes, the **nature** of the information which is needed changes as well. Policy makers might wish to know if I.Q. tests "work," if they are cheap, if they can identify "gifted children."

On the other hand, a teacher may wish for information on a special strategy to use on Monday with Johnny Jones. A prescriptive diagnosis and a

---

[3]B.C. Gallager, (ed.), NAACP Report on Minority Testing. (New York: NAACP Special Contribution Fund, May 1976).

113

policy recommendation probably required different information, or information at different levels of refinement. Yet the teacher and the policy maker are most likely to get the same information, a raw I.Q. score or scores or a gross label such as "EMR."

Current school uses of I.Q. tests tend to reflect an emphasis on "prediction" and/or "diagnosis." The I.Q. test is supposed to tell us what a child's future school performance will be and, by implication, what the limits of a child's performance must be. The I.Q. test is supposed to tell us what is "broken," "disabled," or "underdeveloped" in the child's thinking process. Both of these uses, **diagnoses** and **prediction**, offer an excellent opportunity to illuminate just how underdeveloped intelligence and I.Q. ideology and practices are.

Let's take them one at a time. I.Q. tests tend to **correlate** positively with other I.Q. tests and with some school grades under certain conditions. Yet other I.Q. tests and school grades both tend to use test items which are quite similar to those on the I.Q. test with which we begin. Therefore, we should not live in awe of the fact that a given thing tends to be mildly associated with something quite like itself. On the other hand, we should be embarrassed as scientists that virtually all of the I.Q. correlations which are reported in the literature are based on many studies that repeat a simple unscientific error. That unscientific error is the failure to **control for known major sources of variation in experimental or general testing conditions**, and to ignore this failure in subsequent interpretation. To be specific, there is an almost universal **failure control for instructional treatment''** in the validity studies which have been done. Studies using pre-measures on I.Q. tests and post-measures on school grades **presume** equivalence of "treatment" or teaching among subjects among comparison groups. Nothing could be further from the truth in most cases in the schools.[4] Moreover, there are compelling data which suggest that if this were done, the famous or infamous I.Q. correlation would evaporate.[5] This seems to be a taboo area for most I.Q. research.

But what about **diagnosis**? The use of the word "diagnosis" implies a knowledge of how thinking **ought** to work. When a professional in **applied** areas such as clinical psychology, school psychology, educational psychology, or school teaching uses the word "diagnosis," there is a further implication. **That implication is that there is a systematic practice or**

[4]Ray Rist, *The Urban School: A Factory for Failure*, (Cambridge, MA: MIT Press, 1973).

[5]Paulo Freire, *Education for Critical Consciousness*. (New York: Seabury, 1973). Renee Fuller, *In Search of the I.Q. Correlation: A Scientific Whodunnit.* (Stony Brook, New York: Ball Stick Bird, 1977).

pedagogy which if properly applied, will work to produce student achievement. In such a teaching model, such systematic pedagogy or "treatment" ought to be **public** professional knowledge and should be endorsed as valid by the profession. Medical doctors might call this "standard procedure." Without valid "standard procedure," any I.Q. "diagnosis" for the applied professional is professionally meaningless and useless. Yet, there are in fact no "standard procedures" for teachers in places where I.Q. tests are in use. **Theories** of teaching do exist in abundance. Many teachers and researchers have described how some teachers function. But educators have yet to recognize or to sanction a set of common **valid pedagogies**. Teacher education is still quite anarchic, and so is common teaching practice. This eliminates even the possibility of another critical matter. That matter is that there be a **valid link between testing and pedagogy**, between I.Q. testing and teaching strategies, between "diagnosis" and "prescription," and between both of these and "healing." Is there anyone here or elsewhere who is willing to stake their professional reputation on a claim that these links can be demonstrated.

Without valid or meaningful prediction, we are left with but one major use of I.Q. tests in education. That use is to **sort** students into categories so that they may be treated in special ways. This assumes that the classifications will yield intellectually homogenous groups of students who can and should be given a unique educational treatment as a group. Note again: this special unique treatment is mysterious. It is implied but never described. Sorting can be accomplished by the use of I.Q. tests. But the same sorting **outcomes** could also be accomplished almost as easily by use of the social class indices of family income, family educational level, and family prestige, and by use of skin color.[6] Any other **arbitrary** marker could be used for sorting to identify a part of the population which is to be excluded from normal opportunity. But this kind of sorting is clearly political, and not psychological or educational in any professional sense.[7] To be professional, the testing and pedagogy link would have to be validated.

---

[6]Ralph Nader, "The Power and the Story of the Educational Testing Service." *The Advocate*. (George Washington University, Feb. 7, 1979), p. 9.

[7]Thomas O. Hilliard, "The Role of Political and Social Action in the Prevention of Psychopathology of Blacks: A Mental Health Strategy for Oppressed People." (University of Vermont, Fifth Conference on the Primary Prevention of Psychopathology, 1979).

Basically then the whole I.Q. test operation rests on three legs. They are:

1. Prediction
2. Diagnosis
3. Sorting

None of these as yet can be regarded as valid educational practice. There are no data to show that student performance is improved because of these three uses of tests.

The I.Q. test may serve well as a clinical interview protocol for a psychologist who is thoroughly familiar with a student's culture. Further I.Q. tests or items should be permitted for purposes of research for test development. I take no issue whatsoever with these uses. It is only when as a clinical aid the I.Q. test is offered as a **"measurement"** device in a scientific sense, or when a research tool is passed off as a valid applied device that the illegitimate imposition of tests on clients must be questioned.

I hope that I have made it clear that it is **not simply the misuse** of currently used I.Q. tests but the **inherent scientific inadequacy** of the tests themselves that is being questioned. Further, I hope that it is also clear that I have made no special plea here for correcting the cultural bias of currently used I.Q. tests. The problem is far more grave than that. The cultural bias only shows us that **standardized mass-produced** "measurement" is impossible when variable cultural material is being **aggregated** in cross-cultural settings. This is aggregating apples and oranges. The culture and measurement issue is a matter of science first and then equity. Clearly, Pandora's box will be opened in the mental measurement laboratory on the very day that cultural anthropologists and socio-linguists are invited to look at what we do. No existing standardized I.Q. test can survive that kind of scientific scrutiny. The whole I.Q. testing movement reflects either an ignorance of or an unwillingness to deal with relevant academic data, especially socio-linguistic. The incomplete literature review in most research on the validation of I.Q. tests will reveal this scientific defect.

If Nero did indeed fiddle while Rome burned, then it is a fitting analogy for I.Q. test advocates and for those who fail to teach children successfully. While test advocates conduct their pseudo "measurements," there are numerous examples of outstanding pedagogy in America and in the world which proceed without them. There are exciting examples which include those where there is dramatic achievement for children who should not have been able to achieve so well, based upon their I.Q. scores.[8] It should be sobering to note that **in my experience with teaching that succeeds, I do not know of a single instance in which the educators or psychologists relied upon I.Q. tests**! The other side of that is this: **I have yet to see a demonstration anywhere to show that the use of I.Q. tests make a positive difference in the achievement of children**. Researchers have looked at every child, family, or social-class variable imaginable, yet the empirical proof of the pedagogical utility of I.Q. tests remains to be done.

In my experience of observing successful teaching and in reviewing the literature on that same subject, I have yet to come across teachers or psychologists who utilize the construct of intelligence directly in their work. They simply do not talk in terms of a **measured** amount of student capacity. I am aware that the systematic observation of learners has begun to help us to understand the teaching and learning process better. Piaget's work seems to have the potential for a growing application in teaching.[9]

The systematic observation of learners over long periods of time and across broad cultural groups will eventually yield basic scientific knowledge, especially when the **unique** patterns of learners are observed, accounted for and interpreted a la Piaget. The spate of publications which deal with the application of Piaget to the classroom, though incomplete and sometimes controversial, may be compared favorably to the relative absence of widely used publications which **spell out the use of "intelligence" and I.Q. in the classroom**. What can a teacher do with "g?" even if it turns out to be more than an artifact of particular approaches to testing and data analysis. When "g" is "measured," what more does a practicing professional know about a child than he or she knew before? Few I.Q. technicians seem to have the courage to go beyond academic fortune telling at about the same level of specificity as our daily horoscopes in the Toonerville Chronicle. There simply is no significantly useful information in the test for teachers.

Intelligence as a construct and currently used I.Q. tests fail education, not merely because of their readily apparent technical poverty, or because of

---

[8]Freire, *Education for Critical Consciousness*; Fuller, *In Search of the I.Q. Correlation: A Scientific Whodunit*; Asa G. Hilliard, III, "Standardization and Cultural Bias: Impediments to the Scientific Study of Intelligence," *Journal of Research and Development in Education*, vol. 12, no. 2, (1979), pp. 47-58; William Johntz, Director Project SEED, Berkely, California, 1976, (Interview).

[9]David Elking, *A Sympathetic Understanding of the Child Six to Sixteen*. (Boston: Allyn and Bacon, 1971). Hans G. Furth, "Intellectual Health in School: What Can Piaget Contribute?" In *Piagetian Theory and its Implications for the Helping Professions*. (Los Angeles: University of Southern California, 1977), pp. 1-12.

demonstrable cultural bias,[10] but because they are, at present, useless as instructional tools.

The repair of the damage which has been done in the quest for I.Q. and intelligence can be made only if work is begun on the right problems! This requires that fundamental confusion be overcome.

1. **Statistical** bias must no longer be confused with **cultural** bias.

To address the issue of cultural bias there must be a sophisticated identification of cultural groups, an understanding of culture and cognition, and an understanding of socio-linguistic principles. The fact that items may appear to "work the same way" within two different "cultural" groups when simple statistical calculations are used does **not** deal effectively with the cultural issue. How are the cultural groups to be identified? How does sample selection proceed?

2. **English** must no longer be confused with **language**. Alas, English is only **a** language. It is only one of many. Even at that it is a polyglot language, made up of a basically Germanic morphology and a basically Romance or Latin vocabulary. Just as with many other linguistic amalgams, it has **utilitarian** value. However, thinking can be expressed in every language. English does not own thinking. Getting English rules "right" is not necessarily the same as getting thinking right. Therefore, the deep structure of language[11] can no longer be confused with the surface structure (a particular language such as English). Standard of "correct" English should no longer be confused as a **unique** expression of thinking. The implications of this for standardized testing which use "standard English" are immense.

3. The **aggregation of numbers** (test scores) must no longer be confused with the aggregation of comparable "units of mental **behavior**." With what logic can a subject's response to a block design item be **aggregated** with a response to a vocabulary item? This is measurement??

4. **Prediction** must no longer be confused with diagnosis. The noting of a small association between two sets of **scores** (I.Q. and achievement) is not an **explanation** of the association.

---

[10]Asa G. Hilliard, "I.Q. Thinking as the Emperor's New Clothes," in *Perspectives on Bias in Mental Testing*, ed. Cecil R. Reynolds and Robert T. Brown (New York and London: Plenum Press), pp. 139-169. (also see pp. 566-572)

[11]Noam Chomsky, *Syntastic Structure*. (The Hague: Mouton, 1957). Claude Levi-Strauss, *The Savage Mind*. (University of Chicago, 1966).

5. **Statistical categories** must no longer be confused with **behavioral functions**.

   For example, a "gifted" person cannot be described simply as a person who "falls into the top 2%" of scores on an I.Q. test. A description of the **unique** mental functions must be made. There is no reason whatsoever for the frequency of **functions** to appear in a population by **prior definition** rather than be actual experience.

6. **Non-discriminatory assessment** must no longer be confused with **valid assessment**.

   The search for "culture free" assessment had to be a failure almost by definition. Virtually all communicative human behaviors appear to be human **creativities**, or simply "cultural" material. Culture **must** be used in all assessment, but not the same culture in all assessment. Further "non-discriminatory" assessment may be politically acceptable but professionally useless, unless it reveals valid information about intelligent behavior for each group to which it is applied. Thus, for example, the pathetic attempt with SOMPA (System of Multicultural Pluralistic Assessment) is almost humorous. It is a hodgepodge of data which would take 50 IBM computers to unravel. The results offer no more to teaching than the I.Q. tests which it was designed to replace or augment. Indeed it even includes one of the I.Q. tests which its author has criticized earlier. Now SOMPA has joined mass production. The construct "adaptive behavior" has even less meaning than "intelligence."

If intelligence really exists in anything like the form which is represented in popular hypotheses, then the future may show something which has yet to be revealed. Varying patterns of thought - perhaps habits of thought would be more accurate - can be observed very readily today. However, the **standardized "measurement"** of mental "potential" or "ability" in either an absolute or a relative sense remains a hope and not a reality. After all the hocus-pocus, I.Q. testing and professional reasoning in education, using intelligence as a construct, tell us little more than a sensitive teacher already knows about a given child.

Educators bought the proverbial "pig-in-a-poke" when I.Q. testing and intelligence ideology were let into the tent. In doing so, they bought a new dependence with a ravenous appetite for resources. It is also a dependent that spends a great deal of time with its own cosmetics but no time at all helping with the housework. It has great fragrance but no substance. Maybe a diet or a fast would help.

Summary:

The standardized I.Q. tests which are in use in the schools are scientifically and pedagogically without merit. The construct "intelligence" is a hypothetical notion whose valid expression has yet to be born. I.Q. tests and the construct of intelligence can be discarded at present, and teaching strategies would be unaffected. To successful teachers the tests are at best a pure nuisance and at worst a reactive influence on teaching and learning. The tests are not simply culturally biased. That bias is only a symptom of the problem which is their scientific inadequacy. To say that "they are the best we have," is not to say that they contribute anything useful at all to instruction. The construct "intelligence" is embryonic and has heuristic value for research. Its utility for instruction remains to be demonstrated. School teachers and students should be relieved of the burden of this bad science and psychological ideology. Test-makers should come again when this product can help to make education better.

The San Francisco Public Schools Experience with Alternatives to I.Q. Testing: A Model for Non-Biased Assessment[1]

by
Harold E. Dent

September 25th, 1986 will be remembered as the day that marked a major milestone in the effort to achieve educational equity for Black children. On that day, Judge Robert F. Peckham, Presiding Judge of the Federal District Court of Northern California signed an order approving a settlement between the Plaintiffs in the Larry P. Case and the California State Department of Education (SDE).[2] This settlement required the SDE to notify all California school districts that standardized individual tests of intelligence (I.Q. tests) could no longer be administered to Black students **for any purpose**.

In his 1979 landmark decision,[3] Judge Peckham found that standardized I.Q. tests were culturally biased because they did not account for the cultural background and experiences of Black children. As a result of that ruling, I.Q. tests could not be given to Black students for the purpose of placing those students in Special Education Classes for the Educable Mentally Retarded (EMR). In the intervening years since 1979, enforcement of the ban on I.Q. tests in public schools in California was virtually non-existent. School districts concocted a myriad of excuses to justify continued use of I.Q. tests, with and without the sanction of SDE officials. However, the 1986 order specifically stipulates, "There is no special education related purpose for which I.Q. tests shall be administered to Black pupils."

For most, if not all, school districts in California this complete prohibition against using I.Q. tests will require major changes in the methods used in the placement of Black student in special education. Traditionally, when a child was suspected of having a problem in learning, the regular class teacher would refer the student for special education placement. The referral was processed and more often than not the child was placed in a special education program. Research indicated that referral almost automatically

---

[1]Special recognition is due to Mrs. Olivia G. Martinez, former Associate Superintendent of Schools, S.F.U.S.D. and Dr. Richard Figueroa, Dept. of Education, U.C. Davis, for their respective roles in the design and development of this program.
[2]No. C-71-2270 RFP, *Order Modifying Judgement*, Sept. 25, 1986.
[3]No. C-71-2270 RFP *Opinion*, Dec. 12, 1979.

resulted in placement.[4] Ysseldyke and Algozzine[5] found that as many as ninety-two percent of referrals for special education placement were confirmed by the school psychologist after administration of an I.Q. test. The practice of routinely administering an I.Q. test to Black students persisted in California even after the 1979 Federal Court Order.[6] I.Q. test usage continues in other states, despite the Larry P. decision, P.L. 94-142[7] and the plethora of research data confirming the cultural bias of commercially developed standardized tests.

The relationship between the use of standardized I.Q. test and the overrepresentation of Black students in special education programs for the educable mentally retarded has been well established.[8] One often hears the testimonial accounts of school psychologists who cite isolated instances of how an I.Q. test score prevented a Black child from being placed in special education. While these accounts may be accurate, they can not offset the statistically documented disproportionate number of Black students inappropriately placed in EMR classes as a result of the use of culturally biased I.Q. tests.

Although most California school districts have purged I.Q. test scores from students' cummulative folders, the San Francisco Unified School District (S.F.U.S.D.) was one of only a few districts to actually comply with the Federal court's ban on I.Q. tests prior to this recent settlement.[9] San Francisco prohibited I.Q. testing for all students in February 1984 following the Appellate Court's original ruling in the Larry P. Case. San Francisco was also the only large school district in California bold enough and courageous enough to accept responsibility and put forth sincere effort to develop an alternative to the traditional method of assessment. The non-biased alternative approach to assessment designed specifically to reduce the overrepresentation of Black and other minority students in special education programs in the S.F.U.S.D. will be described in the following pages, as initially developed and proposed by Richard Figueroa.

This article is prepared to serve a threefold purpose. First, it is intended to provide an accurate description of a complex program that has real

---

[4]Mercer, J.R. *SOMPA Technical Manual*, The Psychological Corporation, New York, 1979.

[5]Ysseldyke, J.E. and Algozinne, B. *Critical issues in special and remedial education.* Boston, Houghton Mifflin, 1982.

[6]No. C-71-2270 RFP 1979 op. cit.

[7]Public Law 94-142, The Education For All Handicapped Children's Act of 1975, requires tests to be selected and administered in a non-discriminatory manner.

[8]Heller, K.A., Holtzman, W.H. and Messick, S. (Editors). *Placing children in special education: A strategy for equity.* National Academy Press, Washington, D.C., 1982.

[9]California State Department of Education, Larry P. compliance monitoring team report, 1986.

potential for providing a fair and appropriate assessment of the educational needs and functional abilities of Black students. Second, it is intended to clarify the misconceptions about the S.F.U.S.D.'s program of non-biased assessment of cognitive behavior. Finally, it is intended to encourage those who are seeking alternative approaches to allow their creativity to explore and experiment with new techniques and to modify existing techniques in their efforts to achieve the goal of non-biased assessment.

The role of the I.Q. test in the disproportionate representation of Black students in special education is well documented.[10] The I.Q. score is unquestionably the most important bit of information gathered in the placement process. To emphasize that point Judge Peckham cited the specific section of the California Ed Code in his decision, which stipulated that the I.Q. score must substantiate all other data such as developmental history, school achievement and adaptive behavior information, etc. While the I.Q. test is tremendously important, the placement actually begins with the initial referral from the regular class teacher. Thus, if we are going to impact the problem of the inappropriate placement of Black students, efforts must be directed toward the referral process, as well as the testing procedures. The non-biased assessment program designed for the San Francisco schools focused on all aspects of the referral process. In order to reduce the overrepresentation of Black students in special education we must reduce the number of false positives that occur in the referral process. Another way of saying this would be that we must reduce the number of Black students who are determined to be eligible for special education when in fact they are not in need of special education services. Figure 1 below graphically portrays this eligibility/need relationship.

Figure 1

	In Need of Spec. Ed.	Not in Need of Spec. Ed.
Eligible for Spec. Ed.	+ +	+ - (False positives)
Not Eligible for Spec. Ed.	- + (False Negatives)	- -

In the eligibility/need paradigm the factors that influence special education placement are, the student's need for special education services **and** his/her

---

[10]No. C-71-2270 RFP, 1979, op. cit.

eligibility for special education services. The relationships between these variables are evident in Figure 1. The combination of two positive categories, "In need" and "Eligible" results in an appropriate placement. The combination of two negative categories, "Not in need" and "Not eligible" results in an appropriate rejection or denial of the placement. The combination of the "In need" and the "Not eligible" categories results in a false negative or a denial of a special education placement, when in fact the student actually needs special education services. There is little data available as to the magnitude and impact of this type of error. However, improved referral and assessment techniques will obviously reduce the number of students in this group and result in more of these students receiving the services they truly need. The combination of the "Not in need" and the "Eligible" categories produces the false positives, the students who are in fact not mentally retarded nor learning disabled, but who are determined to be eligible for special education and are ultimately (inappropriately) placed. It is highly probable that the students in this false positive group are in need of some form of supplemental educational services. They are usually functioning well below grade level. But, if there is no evidence of a handicapping condition or learning disability, the supplemental services they need should be provided through the regular education program.

The San Francisco program of non-biased assessment was designed specifically to reduce or eliminate the false positives in the placement process. When this program was introduced into the S.F.U.S.D. in the Spring of 1984, Black enrollment in special education was two and one half times the Black enrollment in the district. Blacks comprised 22.1% of the district population, but in those special education categories where there was no organic basis for the placement decision, Blacks were grossly overrepresented: Educable Mentally Retarded 46.1%; Special Day Classes 41.7%; Special Learning Disabilities 63.5%; and Resource Specialist Program 49.7%. This disproportionate enrollment of Blacks was more or less typical of large school districts in California at the time. Of interest is the fact that throughout the State of California and the nation, Black enrollment in classes for the Trainable Mentally Retarded (TMR) or Severely Mentally Retarded is and always has been consistently comparable to the Black enrollment in the district. The percentage of Black students enrolled in the TMR program in San Francisco in 1984 was 22.3%.

A Program of Non-discriminatory Assessment

This program was designed specifically to assist the I & A (Identification and Assessment) staff of the Special Education Department of the San Francisco Unified School District evaluate the educational needs and functional abilities of students referred for special education placement. The program offered a research based, theoretical framework within which to gather, analyze and interpret the necessary information needed to formulate a professional opinion and/or decision concerning the student's need and eligibility for special education services. In compliance with the January 1984 affirmation by the U.S. Appellate Court of Judge Peckham's ban on I.Q. tests, the Associate Superintendent for Special Services prohibited the use of standardized I.Q. tests for all special education placements. Once before a similar prohibition on I.Q. tests had been issued by the California State Board of Education following Judge Peckham's 1974 preliminary injunction. However, that decision was unceremoniously rescinded prior to the 1979 permanent injunction.

The key features of this non-biased approach to cognitive assessment are that: 1) the assessment is conducted without the use of standardized psychometric tests; 2) the presence of a handicapping condition or learning disability must be documented; and, 3) emphasis of this approach is on the process of learning rather than on the product of learning (as represented by a score on a psychometric test). The foundations for actual assessment of intellective functions in this proposed program are found in the research in cognition of information processing,[11] particularly the research documenting differences in the information processing behavior of retarded and non-retarded learners.[12]

This model for a process of non-biased cognitive assessment is composed of six separate stages. Although these stages are sequential, it is not necessary to go through all stages with each child. In fact, it is anticipated that as the data is gathered at each stage many students will be determined to be ineligible and therefore, only a small number of those referred will be carried through the entire six stage process. In other words, a child's assessment can be discontinued at any stage because the problem has been resolved by appropriate intervention or explained by other factors.

---

[11]Sternberg, R.J. (Editor). *Handbook of human intelligence.* Cambridge University Press, New York, 1982.

Sternberg, R.J. (Editor). *Human abilities: An information processing approach*, W.H. Freeman and Co., New York, 1985.

[12]Campione, J.C., Brown, A.L. and Ferrara, R.A. Mental retardation and intelligence, in Sternberg (Ed.), *Handbook of human intelligence.*

THE SIX STAGE MODEL FOR
NON-DISCRIMINATORY ASSESSMENT

1. MONITORING THE SPECIAL EDUCATION REFERRALS BY ETH-
   NICITY, AGE, SEX AND HANDICAPPING CONDITION IN CLASS-
   ROOMS, SCHOOLS, DISTRICT AREAS AND TESTERS.
2. ASSESSING THE REFERRAL DATA AS WELL AS ALL OTHER
   SCHOOL DATA AVAILABLE ON THE PARTICULAR STUDENT TO
   SEE IF IN FACT THE "PROBLEM" HAS BEEN CONSISTENTLY
   NOTED AND HAS BEEN PERVASIVE ACROSS SEVERAL SETTINGS.
3. MODIFYING THE INSTRUCTIONAL PROGRAM OF THE STUDENT
   TO SEE IF THE "LEARNING PROBLEM" CAN BE RESOLVED
   THROUGH SUCH MODIFICATIONS OF THE REGULAR
   CURRICULUM.
4. EVALUATING THE STUDENT'S PRESENT INSTRUCTIONAL PRO-
   GRAM BOTH AS IT EFFECTS ALL THE STUDENTS IN THAT
   CLASS AND THE PARTICULAR STUDENT UNDER
   CONSIDERATION.
5. ASSESSING THE CHILD'S HOME CURRICULUM AND HIS/HER
   LEARNING ABILITY WITHIN IT.
6. ESTIMATING THE STUDENT'S LEARNING ABILITY IN THE REG-
   ULAR SCHOOL PROGRAM, AND/OR IN THE MODIFIED REGU-
   LAR SCHOOL PROGRAM, AND/OR IN A CLINICAL LEARNING
   SITUATION TO DETERMINE WHETHER THERE IS A LEARNING
   HANDICAP THAT WILL REQUIRE SPECIAL EDUCATION.

At each stage in this process there are considerations that the individu-
al(s) responsible for gathering the data for the assessment should take into
account. The responsibility for completing the assessment is assigned to
different individuals in different districts. Many times it is assigned to more
than one person in the district, e.g., the guidance worker gathers one type of
data, the resource specialist another and the school psychologist another. In
light of the fact that different types of data are gathered at each stage of this
model, we will refer to the individual responsible for gathering the data as
the assessor. Nevertheless, a few of the considerations referred to earlier will
be mentioned briefly in the discussion of each stage of the model.

1. MONITORING THE SPECIAL EDUCATION REFERRALS AND
   PLACEMENTS BY ETHNICITY, AGE, SEX AND HANDICAPPING
   CONDITION IN CLASSROOMS, SCHOOLS, DISTRICT AREAS AND
   TESTERS.

This stage of the model does not involve individuals directly. Nevertheless, it could represent a crucial safeguard against misplacement. Every

school district maintains and reports ethnic, age, and gender distributions by compiling this demographic information from each class in each school in the district. Usually these data are gathered and stored in the district's computerized data processing system. The enrollment data of special education classes and other special programs are or should also be maintained in this system. Implementing this first stage of the model will require the incorporation of referral, testing and placement information into the existing data processing system. Once the data has been entered into the system, it should then be possible to continuosly monitor referrals and placements to determine when significant and/or unexpected disparities occur. Expected rates of handicapping conditions can be estimated from any one of several sources. For example, in most districts the ethnic distribution of the TMR (Trainable Mentally Retarded) program usually mirrors the ethnic composition of the district. Although straight percentages might be too stringent, they could be used as first-alert indices. Other criteria can be used to determine when an over or an underrepresentation in any one of the specially funded programs (i.e., special education or programs for the gifted and talented) occurs. The Larry P. settlement accepts the "E" formula,[13] the formula adopted in the Diana v. California settlement, to determine the acceptable percentage of an ethnic group in the district's special education program.

$$E = A + \sqrt{\frac{A(100 - A)}{N}}$$

According to Judge Peckham's *order and memorandum* in Diana, these criteria are not quotas. They are strict guidelines to protect against misdiagnosis and misplacements through careful monitoring the sources of referrals (teachers, schools, areas) and placements (testers and IEP teams) in order to insure that ethnic, age or gender disparities in the rate of handicapping conditions are not produced by systemic causes.

Implementing this stage of the model will involve the design of special data processing programs so that referrals, testing and placement information can be accessed immediately. If at all possible, some form of baseline data

---

[13]where A = Percent of ethnic group in district population.
  N = No. of students in special education
  E = Acceptable percentage of ethnic groups in EMR.
Diana v. State Board of Education C-70-37 RFP, Jan. 18. 1979.

should be collected which includes ethnic, age and gender percentages in the district by areas, schools and classes. The expected percentages or acceptable percentages of pupils in the various special education categories should also be included in the data processing program. If available, the percentages of students who are referred, tested and placed in special education programs over the last three year period could be entered into the computerized system. Ideally, this would permit comparison of the annual patterns of referrals and placements that have occurred during the last three years with those patterns that will emerge from this new approach to cognitive assessment.

2. ASSESSING THE REFERRAL DATA AS WELL AS ALL OTHER SCHOOL DATA AVAILABLE ON THE PARTICULAR STUDENT TO SEE IF IN FACT THE "PROBLEM" HAS BEEN CONSISTENTLY NOTED AND HAS BEEN PERVASIVE ACROSS SEVERAL SETTINGS.

"Assessment of the referral data" means consulting with the teacher to determine the specific behaviors that indicated to the teacher that the pupil is handicapped and in need of special education services. Specificity of the observations of the behavior is crucial since this process facilitates verification of any history of this or similar problems in the pupil's prior learning experiences. Interviews with previous teachers should be held to see if the problem(s) was/were noted earlier. Written records of the detailed descriptions of the behavior by the teachers should be maintained, with notation of the verification or lack of verification by others.

A detailed review of the student's academic files should also be undertaken. Grades, test results, anecdotal information, and any other data should be summarized and profiled. Again, the attempt here is to verify the present, observed problem(s). Where such verification is not available, the assessor has two options: either to stop the referral process and consult with the teacher to refine and/or record additional observations of the child's behavior or proceed to stage three.

3. MODIFYING THE INSTRUCTIONAL PROGRAM OF THE STUDENT TO SEE IF THE "LEARNING PROBLEM" CAN BE RESOLVED THROUGH SUCH MODIFICATIONS OF THE REGULAR PROGRAM.

Public Law 94-142 (The Education For All Handicapped Children's Act) requires that before a student is referred for special education assessment, he/she should have the regular education program modified. In actual practice, such modifications are seldom carried out in a systematic, controlled manner. The assessor or the child study team usually makes general recommendations to the referring teacher but seldom assumes direct responsibility for monitoring the changes recommended or their impact on the student's learning. This stage of the model requires that the assessor or the child study team undertake a fairly detailed investigation of the student's problem(s) and make specific recommendations as to how the instructional program can be modified to meet the needs of that particular student. Further, the assessor/team should closely monitor the impact of these modifications, carefully documenting the results of these modifications on the pupil's behavior and learning. The modifications should be clearly described. The relevance of the modifications to the child's problem(s) should also be clearly stated, as well as the differences between the modifications and the regular program.

The modifications should begin with the most unobtrusive set of possible changes (changing seating arrangements, peer tutoring, structured work for a given period of time with the teacher, etc.) and proceed to more intense interventions (tutoring outside the class, instruction by a reading specialist, etc.). Ideally, every school should have a list of such possible modifications. Also, where there are unique characteristics in the student population, the menu of modifications should reflect awareness of these unique characteristics (e.g. cultural lifestyles or linguistic patterns).

When a student begins to demonstrate positive changes in the perceived problem, the assessor or the team should prepare a plan for implementing the salutory aspects of these modifications in the regular program. The assessor/team should then be available to assist the teacher implement these modifications permanently or as long as they elicit the desired benefits. The principal of the school should participate in this process in order to provide support and resources to the teacher.

Throughout this process, the parents should be actively engaged in helping the student. At a minimum, the parents should be kept informed of the modifications and of the student's progress or lack of progress throughout these changes in program.

4. EVALUATING THE STUDENT'S PRESENT INSTRUCTIONAL PROGRAM AS IT EFFECTS ALL THE STUDENTS IN THE CLASS AND THE PARTICULAR STUDENT UNDER CONSIDERATION.

This stage of the model is taken directly from the National Academy of Sciences' report on *Placing Children In Special Education: A Strategy For Equity*.[14] The report suggests that a child's academic achievement test scores as well as those of his/her peers be used to gauge the level of working performance of the class. In essence, this means establishing a standard against which to judge the student's present problems and the impact of the instructional program on the entire class. This is probably one of the most

---

[14]Heller, Holtzman & Messick, *op. cit.*

controversial aspects of the Academy's report. It is, in essence, an evaluation of the learning environment in which the student's problems have been noted. Assessing the quality of the classroom program places the assessor in a precarious position if one views this recommendation as an invitation to indict or blame the teacher. In the present model, this stage suggests neither of these views.

In this stage, the assessor sets out to determine whether there is a disordinal interaction between the pupil's characteristics and; the group of children in the class, the level of prior knowledge expected from the students, the rate of learning required, the language style of instruction used, the level of structure and direction given the students as they are presented with new material, etc. The focus is on the interaction between what the student brings and what the class offers.

If the assessor finds there is a disordinal interaction, or if the assessor finds that the teacher needs help in the instructional process, the relationship between the assessor and the teacher should then become a collaborative or consultative relationship. Both work together to change and, if necessary, enhance the learning environment. The assessor/consultant should provide support, encouragement and, where possible, resources. Sanctions or negative evaluations should not be expressed. The most that can happen is that the assessor/consultant could recommend a change of classroom for the student being assessed.

The observations of the student in the classroom as well as the observations of the entire instructional setting and climate should be extensive and carefully documented. Care should be taken to insure that whatever is noted has been consistently observed. Particular attention should be given to the amount of time-on-task the student typically averages during the various academic lessons and tasks, and the relationship of this individual's average to the classroom average of time-on-task.

There should be evidence of a clear and persistent disparity between the student's level of achievement in that class and that of his/her peers. The disparity could be either comprehensive (such as in the case of mental retardation) or unique to specific academic activities (such as in specific learning disabilities). Further, the disparity should not be evident in other students having similar backgrounds or linguistic characteristics as those of the student in question. In this situation, curricular or structural changes are called for, other than those required when there is a handicapping condition.

5. ASSESSING THE CHILD'S HOME CURRICULUM AND HIS/HER LEARNING ABILITIES WITHIN IN.

This stage of the model requires that the assessor visit the student's home. The visitor to the pupil's home should have at least three goals in mind. First, they should make a determination of the degree of cultural and linguistic differences. Special emphasis should be paid to the differences between the child's home curriculum and that of the school. Second, they should try to determine the degree and type of "mediated learning experiences"[15] that characterize the interactions between the child and the primary caretakers. This is particularly important in homes where the acculturation patterns generate differences in child-rearing practices, expectations, aspirations and communication styles. Third, they should elicit information from the primary caretakers as to the learning abilities of the child in the acquisition of self-maintenance and culturally appropriate behaviors (i.e., adaptive behaviors).

All of the data gathered during the home visits should be directed toward answering the question, Is there any evidence that the parents have noted that the child has difficulties in learning, difficulties that are related to those described in the teacher's referral symptoms?

6. ESTIMATING THE STUDENT'S LEARNING ABILITIES IN THE REGULAR SCHOOL PROGRAM, AND/OR IN THE MODIFIED REGULAR PROGRAM, AND/OR IN A CLINICAL LEARNING SITUATION TO DETERMINE WHETHER THERE IS A LEARNING HANDICAP THAT WILL REQUIRE SPECIAL EDUCATION.

As the National Academy Report suggests, relatively few children should make it to this stage. It is at this juncture that the assessor must make direct observations of the child engaged in the process of learning. Two broad possibilities for doing this are available to the assessor. The assessor could directly observe the student while the teacher instructs him/her in the regular class program or in the modified program (referred to in step three). Or the assessor could observe the student in a clinical learning situation through the application of current cognitive assessment techniques.[16] The movement to understand human abilities in terms of information processing has spawned a variety of techniques and approaches designed to assess cognitive behavior.

The information processing movement grew from the cognitive theorists' dissatisfaction with the emphasis of the psychometric approach which

---

[15]Feuerstein, R. *The Dynamic assessment of retarded performers.* University Park Press, Baltimore, 1979.

[16]Budoff, M. *Learning potential and educability among the educable mentally retarded*, Final Report Project No. 312. Cambridge, Mass., Research Institute for Educational Problems, 1974.

Vigotsky, L.S. *Mind in society: the development of higher psychological processes.* In N. Cole, V. John-Steiner, S. Scribner and E. Souberman, (eds.), Cambridge, Mass. Harvard University Press, 1978.

Feuerstein, R. 1979, op. cit.

Jones, R.L. *Non-discriminatory assessment of minority group children: a casebook.* In press.

focuses on the end product of learning, the score on a psychometric test. Information processing seeks to understand human intelligence in terms of the mental processes that underlie observable behavior. According to Sternberg, cognitive assessment is not only feasible, but quite likely more effective and valid than the traditional psychometric assessment conducted with I.Q. tests.[17] The conceptual framework for the clinical/cognitive assessment will be discussed in the following section.

The data gathered in this referral process, including the data from the clinical/cognitive assessment, will not yield quantitative units or scores that can be translated into a classification such as in the case of mental retardation (an I.Q. score below 70). The determination of eligibility for special education placement in this process model is based on the documentation of a pervasive pattern of behavior that confirms for the assessor or enables the assessor to conclude that a learning problem or a handicapping condition exists. The ultimate responsibility for determining eligibility of a student for special education placement under this model rests on the professional judgement of the assessor.

The Clinical/Cognitive Assessment

Stages one through five of this process model describes the mechanisms for gathering all the data that school administrators, theoreticians and practitioners agree are necessary to complete an assessment of a student being considered for special education placement, except for the clinical /cognitive assessment data documenting the presence of a handicapping condition or learning disability. The sixth stage provides the theoretical framework and suggests certain techniques which can be employed to conduct the assessment of the student's cognitive behavior.

In the design and implementation of this program the planners recognize the need to comply with the requirements of the Federal Court Order and the need to insure the scientific and professional credibility of this effort. The requirements of the court that tests used in the placement of students be non-discriminatory and be validated for the purpose for which they were used essentially eliminated all commercially developed, standardized tests of intelligence. Publishers and test makers' claims notwithstanding, there are not standardized tests of intelligence on the market that meet those requirements. It is a well established fact that the standardization process itself

---

[17]Sternberg, R.J. 1985, *op. cit.*

represents a significant source of bias.[18] The fact that Blacks, and other minorities, comprise only small segments of the standardization sample is evidence that the impact of Black culture and other minority cultures will be negligible in the standardization process. Moreover, there are no commercially developed, standardized tests that have been validated for the specific purpose of placing Black students in special education programs.

The question of the validity of a single test or instrument used in this assessment is moot, because the techniques employed in this assessment process do not yield the quantitative data necessary to apply a statistical test of validity.

The issue of the scientific and professional credibility of the program rests on the fact that the foundations of the techniques and concepts used in this system are rooted in research that documents differences between the performance of retarded and non-retarded learners, and includes research with other children having difficulties in school and test situations.[19] In an extensive review of research in cognition, Campione, Brown and Ferrara,[20] have identified specific determinants of performance which differentiates mildly retarded learners from their non-retarded counterparts. The Campione, Brown and Ferrara article, like the six stage assessment process proposed for San Francisco, was intended to improve diagnosis and remediation, not classification.[21]

Determinants of Performance

The areas of intellective performance in which the retarded and the non-retarded have been found to differ are: A) the speed or efficiency with which elementary information processing operations are carried out; B) the student's knowledge base or the extent and organization of relevant knowledge available to the learner; C) the role of strategies for dealing with memory and problem solving situations; D) metacognition, the subject's understanding of his/her cognitive processes; and E) executive control; the choice, timing, sequencing and monitoring of cognitive activities. The reader is cautioned that these determinants should not be considered as

---

[18]Green, D.R. *Racial and ethnic bias in test construction*, Final Report of the U.S. Office of Education Contract No. OEC 9-70-0058 (057) 1972.

Dent, H.E. Assessing black children for mainstream placement, in Jones, R.L. (Ed.) *Mainstreaming and the minority child*. Council for Exceptional Children, Reston, Va. 1976.

Jones, R.L. *Non-discriminatory assessment of minority group children: A casebook*. In press.

[19]Campione, Brown & Ferrara, 1982, *op. cit.*

[20]*Ibid.*

[21]*Ibid.*

independent factors. It must be emphasized that performance in any of these areas is dependent upon the interaction of two or more determinants.

A. This first determinant of performance is speed or efficiency of elementary information processing operations. Performance in many complex domains is interactive, and in order for an interactive system to operate smoothly the different components of the system must operate efficiently. If one of the components of this system operates slowly or inefficiently, then the entire system must suffer. The total operation is slow or less efficient. For example, functional memory skills (e.g., short term memory) are greatly influenced by speed or efficiency of processing, if memory skills are inefficient many learning activities will be affected. Briefly summarized, the research literature indicates that the mildly retarded are less efficient in their execution of simple mental operations.

B. Knowledge Base refers to the extent and organization of the relevant information the student has available to him/her in some domain, and how effectively the student uses that knowledge. In other words, how does that knowledge influence other components of the system? Do retarded children know less than non-retarded children of comparable age because they process information slowly or because they lack the strategic devices and the control of those devices necessary to overcome the limitations? The data suggests that retarded children are less likely to use the information that they are known to have.

C. The role of strategies in the differentiation of retarded learners from non-retarded learners has been explored extensively in the laboratory. Much of the research in this area involves training studies in which the test-teach-test paradigm has been employed. In this procedure baseline information is supplemented by data on the subject's performance after training. The test-teach-test method is suggested as an appropriate means of gathering the data in the clinical/cognitive assessments employed in the proposed program. In the research studies reviewed, this technique was built into the experimental design for theoretical reasons, not for purposes of remediation.

Extensive review has led to consistent findings concerning the use of task appropriate strategies by the retarded. It is generally accepted that school-like problems require some planful, active processing for optimal performance. The first of these conclusions drawn from the research is that when confronted with tasks requiring strategic interventions, the retarded fail to spontaneously employ the necessary strategies and consequently perform poorly. In other words, the retarded do not impose organization on material to be learned. However, it was also found that when trained to employ specific strategies the retarded improved their performance significantly.

Two important findings of this research which theorists believe to be critical to an index of intelligence and that the retarded students were unable to profit from incomplete instructions and failed to transfer learned strategies beyond the original training situations. They were able to maintain a high level of performance once they had learned a strategy as long as the task remained the same. But there was no evidence of transfer to new tasks.

D. Metacognition refers to one's knowledge of one's own cognitive processes and to the active monitoring, sequencing and orchestrating of these processes. These represent two distinct functions, the monitoring and regulating functions are referred to as the executive aspects of cognitive behavior. Metacognition is concerned with the student's knowledge of his/her own cognitive resources and his/her understanding of himself/herself as a learner.. Is the student aware that he/she learns material "A" more easily than material "B"? Can he/she describe how he/she learns "A"? The research studies summarized by Campione, Brown & Ferrara found that educable retarded children were not as insightful about their memory skills as their non-retarded counterparts. They were not as aware of the severity of working-memory limitations and were not as cognizant of the content of their memory as non-retarded children of comparable chronological age.

E. The executive control functions of overseeing, managing and evaluating cognitive behavior are considered by cognitive theorists to be more central to the notion of intelligence and therefore more important as a determinant of intellectual functioning. The evidence in support of the relative importance of executive control was that instructing students about aspects of their cognitive system produced less improvement in performance than instructing them in executive or self-management routines.

Another aspect of this theoretical framework for clinical/cognitive assessment emanates from the advances in research in clinical assessment in Soviet Russia around the concept of the zone of proximal development.[22] According to Vigotsky, the zone of proximal development is the distance between

---

[22]Vygotsky, 1978, *op. cit.*

Brown, A.L. & French, L.A. The zone of potential development: Implications for intelligence testing in the year 2000 in Sternberg, R.J. and Detteman, D.K. (Eds.), *Human Intelligence*, Abilex Publishing Corp., Norwood, N.J., 1979).

the child's actual development level as measured by problem solving and the level of potential development achieved on the same task after aid. The zone of proximal development is an estimate of the student's learning potential. it is Vigotsky's contention that the major difference between the learning disabled and the truly mentally retarded learner lies in the width of the zone of proximal development. The degree of aid or amount of intervention needed to assist the child reach a solution or progress along the continuum of learning is an indication of the width of the zone of proximal development. It is reported that the learning disabled child and the mentally retarded child tend to perform similarly in terms of their starting competence on a variety of tasks. However, the two groups differ dramatically in terms of their ability to benefit from additional cues provided by the assessor. The learning disabled need fewer prompts than the retarded before they arrive at a satisfactory solution. They, the learning disabled, were also found to be more proficient at transferring the results of their learned solutions to new situations.

These areas of differential performance styles and the concept of the zone of proximal development were presented as a conceptual framework within which the assessor could gather, analyze and interpret data about the cognitive behavior of students and ultimately to determine the student's need for and eligibility for special education services. As a means of gathering this data, it was recommended that the S.F.U.S.D. provide its staff with training in the use of Learning Potential Assessment Device (LPAD), a system of cognitive assessment designed by Reuven Feuerstein.[23] The LPAD is based on Feuerstein's theory of Structural Cognitive Modifiability, which holds that inadequate cognitive development can be modified through appropriate mediation to improve cognitive functioning. The LPAD will enable the assessor to determine how accessible the child's cognitive behavior is to modification. Modification is accomplished through effective application of mediation (mediated learning experiences). The degree and quality of mediation required to modify the student's cognitive behavior will assist in determining the presence and/or nature of the learning problem, and will assist in formulating recommendations for remediation in the classroom. (A detailed discussion of the Learning Potential Assessment Device appears elsewhere in this issue.)

The data gathered through this assessment process is not only generated from several sources, the teacher, the parents and the student but, it will yield information that will in turn be useful to each of them. It is suggested

---

[23]*Ibid.*

that any formal evaluation compiled from analysis of this data should include a set of recommendations for each of the key players in this scenario. For the teacher the recommendations should focus on remediation strategies found effective in the assessment sessions that could be applicable in the class-room. For the parents the recommendations should include suggested media-tions that can be applied in the home, i.e., mediation of a feeling of competence.[24] For the student the recommendations should focus on the student's responsibility for his/her own behavior, i.e., study habits.

Dissentors in the San Francisco schools, with encouragement from others in the professional psychological community, have been successful, through intimidation and misrepresentation, in bringing a halt to this program before the appropriate data could be compiled to determine the validity of the process. Nevertheless, the application of this approach has been successful in another school district[25] in reducing the overrepresentation of Blacks in special education in one semester by twenty-two percent. Blacks comprised three point five percent (3.5%) of the district population but comprised almost nine percent (8.7%) of the special education pro-grams. After application of this assessment process in the evaluation of less than one-third of the Black students in special education, Black enrollment has been reduced to seven point one percent (7.1%). This reduction of twenty-two percent resulting from the assessment of one-third of the Black student special education population is likely, all other things being equal, to result in an overall reduction of Black enrollment of sixty-six percent (66%) if all Black students were assessed, which is consistent with Mercer's[26] findings and re-evaluation programs conducted in other cities.[27]

The program described in the preceding pages was developed in response to a specific situation, the Federal Court ban on standardized IQ tests. The conditions that prompted that ban, the use of culturally biased testing procedures, and the resulting disproportionate representation of Blacks and other minorities in special education programs, still exist in other school districts across the country where there are sizeable minority populations. It is intended that this and other articles in this issue will encourage school administrators, school board members and parents to examine and challenge the policies, procedures and practices that create inequities in the educa-tional opportunities provided Black and other minority students in our public education system.

[24]*Ibid.*

[25]Dent, H.E. Report of Non-biased Assessment program of S.M.U.S.D., 1985.

[26]Mercer, J.R. *Labelling the Mentally Retarded.* Berkeley, University of California Press, 1973.

[27]Dent, H.E. & Williams, R.L. Association of Black Psychologists Position Paper on psychological Testing, 1972, unpublished manuscript.

The Chicago Public Schools Experience with Alternatives to I.Q. Testing: The Color of Rubies

by
Patricia Heaston

In 1975 in Chicago, Illinois, P.A.S.E. (Parents in Action on Special Education) vs. Hannon was filed on behalf of minority students whose placement in classrooms for the mentally handicapped (E.M.H.) were said to have been based on tests that were culturally biased. When the court decided in 1980 that the tests themselves were not biased, the case, in effect, began in earnest.

From one perspective, the "Chicago experiment"[1] may have had its beginning in the courtroom when it was noted that one black child thought the question on an I.Q. test regarding the color of rubies, referred to a woman's name. The concerns of bias in testing and efficacy of special education appeared to peak and merge in a system where legal, political, and social factors have always had considerable impact on the educational system.

BACKGROUND: A. Craniometry and Beyond

At the core of the issue, though rarely articulated, were the questions of genetic inferiority and institutional racism. When attempts to measure cognitive abilities began to support theories of a racial hierarchical structure, strange and exotic yardsticks began to come into use. The measuring and weighing of skulls and the subsequent comparison of the different races on these bases are embarrassing but undeniable chapters in the history of psychology. The social uses and misuses of mental measurements had begun. Although it may be tempting to believe that the psycho-ethnic problems reached their zenith in the civil rights struggle of the 60's, it is significant to note that early 20th century studies attempting to substantiate a racial superiority were scientifically challenged in the 20's and 30's. One interesting study (1897: Stetson) was made on the memorization of four stanzas. Black students excelled and it was therefore determined that memory was not a valid measurement of intelligence. In 1928, Albert Beckham, who was the first Black psychologist in the Bureau of Child Study, "produced evidence that median I.Q. scores of Black children from Washington, D.C., Baltimore and New York City fell well into the range of

---

[1]H. Carl Haywood personal correspondence.

[2]G.R. Stetson, "*Some Memory Tests of Whites and Blacks*", Psych. Review 4 (1897)

average intelligence. Beckham's investigation countered evidence by white psychologists which had shown that the black child was at least ten points below the white child in I.Q. score level."[3]

Martin Jenkins, in his dissertation at Northwestern University (1936) demonstrated that despite expectations to the contrary, Black children were shown to have a gifted population proportionally the same as whites when **equal educational opportunities were provided**. What is particularly noteworthy, though seldom reported, is that the highest I.Q. on record at the time was achieved by a black girl (I.Q. 200).[4] Given this undeniably substantive work, it is surprising that much more attention and weight were given to subsequent works (Shuey, 1966; Jensen, 1969)[5] which reinforced earlier perceptions of innate inferiority.

Another body of work that received scant attention, yet should have had considerable impact on future research, was the affective components in the psychological evaluation of minority students. In 1928, Herman Canady researched the significance of establishing rapport with black children in the examination process. The possibility that there were other factors to be considered that had significant effects on the examination process when Black children were being evaluated (i.e., race of examiner, motivation, outcome anxiety, locus of control) constituted critical areas for research.

The results of these studies have not enjoyed wide circulation in the broader educational settings and, therefore, have not been appropriately absorbed for utilization. Other factors, particularly those relating to racial identification and self-concept may also have a critical impact on the assessment and education of a Black child. If it is true that "racial awareness is present in Negro children as young as three years old,"[6] then it may also follow that the child's sense of identity will be threatened when he "begins to feel that the color of his skin, the background of his parents, or the fashion of his clothes rather than his wish and his will to learn will decide his worth..."[7] One astute black college student proposed another stage in Erikson's eight stages of development — that of racial awareness.

---

[3]Robert V. Guthrie. *Even the Rat Was White*. Harper Row 1976

[4]M.D. Jenkins, *"A Socio-Psychological Study of Negro Children of Superior Intelligence."* Journal of Negro Ed. 5 (1936)

[5]A.M. Shuey, *The Testing of Negro Intelligence*. New York, Social Science Press 1966; A.R. Jensen, *"How Much Can We Boost I.Q. and Scholastic Achievement"*. Harvard Educational Review. 1969

[6]Kenneth Clark, *Prejudice and Your Child*, Beacon Press 1955

[7]Erik Erikson, *Childhood and Society*, Norton, 1963

The awkwardness with which scholars approach the issue of racism does not diminish the necessity for confronting it. What does this have to do with the tests and testing? It is a factor that needs to be considered when evaluating test outcomes and the social issues therefrom. Joseph White stated: "The psychosocial reality of oppression, based on an abundance of concrete evidence is what prevents Black children from feeling realistically confident that by putting forth a sufficient amount of effort they have a solid chance of achieving a wide range of options."[8] There has been a considerable amount of caution exercised when suggesting there may be differences; however subtle, in the approach to, and products from, mental testing of Black children. On the one hand, it has been held that "the Black child is not deficient in motivation to struggle, to grow, to excel, and to achieve; the deficiency is in the structure of institutional racism built into the fabric of American society."[9]

On the other hand, if the particular perspectives of Black culture and experience values are taken into account in testing or instruction and if the **affective** domain "which appears to be strong in the Black Child"[10] is balanced and tapped along with the cognitive, the concomitant confidence and support necessary to foster learning in multicultural settings, will be facilitated. Any model therefore purporting to address issues relating to the attempts to eliminate bias or to look at students from a multicultural perspective, must take into account the data gleaned from history, and insights gained from contemporary research.

B. From Larry P. to Bigger T

In 1969 the Bay Area psychologists pleaded the California courts to enjoin the system to ban culturally biased I.Q. tests in the determination of mental retardation of Black students. In 1972 a class action suit was filed on behalf of all Black San Francisco school children categorized as Educable Mentally Retarded (E.M.R.) as the results of scores from I.Q. tests. Judge Peckham issued a preliminary injunction in favor of the plaintiffs restraining them from placing Black students in classes for the mentally retarded. The final decision was to ban permanently the use of I.Q. tests in the placement of Black children in mentally retarded classes in the state of California. The temptation to replicate the Larry P. case in Chicago was irresistible. In Chicago, all the elements of the earlier issues were present, in addition to

---

[8]Joseph White. *The Psychology of Blacks: An Afro-American Perspective*, Prentice Hall 1984
[9]IBID
[10]Deryl Hunt, *"Reflections on Racial Perspectives."* Contemporary Black Issues in Social Psychology, 1975

persistent concerns relating to overrepresentation of Blacks in classrooms for mentally handicapped; the place of tests in the decision/placement process; the fairness of the tests themselves; legislative imperatives, and the effectiveness of special education.

The psycho-social and economic circumstances existing in Chicago for Bigger Thomas, the Black boy fictionalized in Richard Wright's *Native Son*, were more complicated three decades later, but in essence remained the same.[11] After receiving a great deal of criticism for appearing to rationalize the rebellious and criminal acts of his protagonist, author Wright indicated in correspondence that he was attempting to portray the "social pressures" on Blacks that differed so dramatically from that of Whites. Chicago in the 1970's was recovering from political attention received in the 1968 convention, the school system was reorganizing and critical attention was being given to the neighborhood school model which reflected a segregated housing pattern. The Coleman Report was highlighting the effects of segregation and integration. The PASE case, originally a class action suit involving Black and Hispanic* students in EMH class-rooms, was initiated in 1974. The premise was basically the same as the Larry P case: to eliminate I.Q. tests as the sole determinant in the consideration of placement of Black (and Hispanic) students in EMH. During the progress of the case (in 1976) Public Law 94-142 was passed, mandating multidisciplinary procedures for assessment and placement and specifying that no single measure could be utilized in the assessment process. The case proceeded, however, and after testimony from several of the witnesses that were involved in Larry P., Judge Grady decided that I.Q. tests were not in and of themselves discriminatory and that sufficient safeguards existed in the federal laws to reduce bias in decision making. Even so, the Chicago Board of Education passed a resolution to voluntarily "discontinue the use of standardized tests in the screening and evaluation of special education (EMH) students and agreed as part of a consent decree, to reassess all EMH students in two years, using a measure possessing local and independent norms. These actions were recommended by consultants to the Chicago Board of Education at that time and placed severe limitations and constraints on the proposed evaluations since there were **no** assessment methods in the general domain which fit these criteria. The consultants recommended that the reassessment proceed by:

(a) using an adaptive behavior scale with independently validated local norms. The ABIC (Adaptive Behavior Inventory of Children) scale

---

[11]Richard Wright, *Native Son*, Harper and Bros., 1940

*The Hispanic representatives later withdrew.

of the SOMPA (System of Multicultural Pluralistic Assessment: Mercer) was suggested.

(b) compliance with Federal and State rules and regulations,

(c) administering traditional I.Q. tests using California norms. (It was suggested the equivalency of California and Chicago norms could be established by contacting minority families by telephone and interviewing them using a sampling of questions for the SOMPA.)

The Chicago Experience

It was clear from the strict parameters set that the mandated task presented an awesome, seemingly impossible, challenge. The first step taken was to survey other states that were given similar directives. There was no district, locale or area that had a model that could be replicated, given the guidelines that had been set. The major stumbling block was the discontinuation of the I.Q. tests combined with a timetable for completion of the reassessment. With the exception of California, most other cities that had to reduce overrepresentation had simply taken an I.Q. score (usually 2 s.d. below the mean = I.Q. 69) and removed all students above this cut-off. Other systems utilized the SOMPA, a combination of the WISC-R and the ABIC adaptive behavior scale, with manipulation of scores to accommodate consideration of family size, structure, and SES; in other words, adjusting scores to compensate for environmental deficits. Since a traditional I.Q. test was at the core of this system, it could not be used.

A Task Force on Nondiscriminatory Assessment and Special Education composed of representation from school councils, institutions of higher education, community agencies, parents and school administration was organized. Responding to the Board consultants, it was noted that (1) assessment procedures had always been closely monitored by Federal and state agencies, (2) using an adaptive scale to substitute for the discontinued intelligence tests would violate legislative guidelines which required that no one instrument be used as a sole criterion for determination for placement. The SOMPA, often mentioned as a substitute, could not be used because it incorporated data from the discontinued WISC-R. (3) Utilizing California norms on a Chicago sample obtained by telephone would discriminate against those families having no telephones and the implications for the application of California norms to a Chicago setting would be highly suspect. The demographic characteristics of a midwestern urban area are disparate enough to make comparisons meaningless.

The pressure to proceed with the reassessment in a reasonable manner considering the legal imperatives but with the needs of the individual students in primary focus, was challenging at best. In 1981 the administrative structure at the Chicago Board of Education underwent a dramatic change, and for the first time in the system's history many of the top administrators, including the Superintendent of Schools, were minority members. The majority of school children in Chicago were Black and the School Board itself had Black representation though not proportionate to the population. The fact that issues of discrimination and lack of equal educational opportunity for Black students were primary concerns of the courts and advocacy groups were of no less significance to the system.

One advocacy group that played a key role in the PASE case and was highly critical of the system, intensified efforts to have the reassessment completed although no additional resources were allocated either in the decision of what assessment techniques to use, or where to secure funds. A recurring model that was suggested several times involved the use of the SOMPA. Champaign, Illinois was recommended as a system whose racial disproportion in EMR had been reduced dramatically. In this system, a plan to reduce the approximately 200 EMH students to 12 by the end of two years involved using an I.Q. cut-off of 69 (2 s.d. below the mean), coupled with an adaptive behavior measure. Because the utilization of I.Q. as a "source of information" was denied by the mandate in Chicago, a different approach had to be used. The State of Illinois had not adopted cut-off scores as a requirement for categorical eligibility. Indeed, the state did not mandate the use of tests at all for categorical determination. It was clear, however, that subjective judgments, even of the highest clinical order, could not be expected to meet standards of objectivity required in such decision-making. With all of the concerns present, there were benefits as well. The major boon for the Chicago system at this time was the climate for change of focus in the assessment process which was indicated from information obtained nationwide.

The Chicago experience occurred at a time and place where considerable thought and effort had been given to the role and functioning of the school psychological services. Almost two decades before, the use and functions of the evaluation process were described as follows:

> "The types of achievement and intelligence tests which are most often used can have only limited value in describing the cognitive functioning of children. In almost all instances we are concerned with scratchings on an answer sheet, not with the ways in which a student arrived at a conclusion. No matter how much we may think we know by looking at scores on such psychometric procedures, unless tests are constructed deliberately to reveal reasoning processes, these processes will not be identified."[12]

---

[12]Susan S. Stodolsky and Gerald Lesser, "Learning Patterns in the Disadvanted" *Harvard Educational Review* V. 37-4, 1967.

For several years the Bureau of Child Study had engaged in research, dialogue, correspondence and inservice training to encourage sensitivity to and awareness of cultural differences and strengths. As the oldest department of school psychological services in the country (1899) there was a commitment to pioneering and innovation in the service of children that made it ideal for investigating new methodologies. The challenge was to focus on retraining a staff that had been academically prepared in traditional assessment modes, and to develop new techniques of observation, strength-assessment and intervention-instruction linkages. Universities were contacted to provide guidance and research input. Professional organizations were alerted to the situation in Chicago and requested to give direction and support. Responses ranged from constructive assistance to "hands-off". A Bureau of Child Study Advisory Board was established which included practitioners and academicians. A Research Division was inaugurated with members reviewing the literature and participating in the standardization of the Kaufman ABC scales. Visits were made to Vanderbilt and Yale universities to investigate the research and practice of a new nondiscriminatory evaluation model. From these sources a comprehensive system began to be conceptualized which recognized the following:

- Measurement of products of learning is most vulnerable to cultural bias.
- Contemporary trends in nondiscriminatory assessment dispute the concept of global identity of intelligence,
- Traditional assessments provide scant information concerning learning process, learning style or learning rate,
- Traditional evaluative techniques yield little information that can be linked to instruction, or that might be amenable to intervention.

In the design and development of the Bureau of Child Study psycho-educational techniques, several other key factors formed the base of the operational philosophy. The lessons of early research were not forgotten: that each ethnic or minority group has proportionately the same range of talent, and that cognitive and affective domains should be tapped. A guiding principle was the need to impact or modify the instructional program based on assessment. Asa Hilliard said:

> "...if you really want to assess a person for the purposes of designing a better instructional environment, and if one aspect of that is to find out what kinds of things a child can do, then the best way of approaching that is to try to teach them and then to see if they learn what you try to teach, and then try again, based on whatever adjustment you would make from what you just learned, and you keep on doing that."[13]

---

[13]Asa Hilliard, *A.P.A. Monitor*, December 1977

It had been said that any assessment that was not linked to intervention was discriminatory. The assessment-intervention link and the effectiveness of the evaluation for instruction purposes provided a foundation for the "process assessment" paradigm adopted by the Bureau. This model was described by Meyers, Pfeffer and Erlbaum. The primary goal of process assessment is "...to determine **how to help** the person being examined."[14]

The purpose of psychological evaluation in this context: (1) to **identify the child's strengths and weaknesses,** and (2) to **develop effective educational and adjustment programs** that can be implemented in the school, home, and the community, on the basis of the evaluation. In this evaluation, the child is viewed as a complex organism that has unique physical/psychological abilities interacting with its unique socio-cultural environment.

The evaluation system emphasizes: (1) **process** rather than outcome, and (2) **modifiability** rather than fixed ability of the child. In order to develop an effective educational program, the underlying learning process involved in arriving at a solution has to be analyzed and understood. Further, the child's learning can be facilitated or improved by teaching strategies. Nondiscriminatory or fair evaluation of the **total child** requires **multifactored assessment**, using multiple strategies of methods for gathering information, on multiple traits or dimensions from multiple sources. Psychologists are required to gather information from all the significant resources including parents, teachers and any other agencies involved with the child, present and past. The major dimensions psychologists assess are: health/medical condition, sensory-motor ability, role behavior at school and home, cognitive skills, socio-cultural background of the family, learning potential, and affective factors. One of the most innovative of the assessment tasks is one in which a student is observed during a task, takes cues from the examiner, and learns from experience. This type of assessment, mentioned specifically in the literature since 1975, focuses on how a student arrives at an answer, determines the learning style and rate, and stresses intervention. Cognitive modifiability, the real possibility of mediating learning and the focus on **process** not product formed the basis of the Bureau of Child Study Psychoeducation Assessment Procedures. A demonstration and two pilot studies were extremely encouraging and supportive of the rationale. Data was collected from a representative sample of all Chicago Public School children for the development of a locally normed nondiscriminatory measure of a student's functioning, in compliance with the specifics of mandates.

---

[14]J. Myers, J. Pfeffer and V. Erlbaum. *Process Assessment. A Model for Broadening the School Psychologist's Assessment Role.* Paper presented at National Association of School of Psychologists, Toronto, March 1982

Concurrent with the design of a new assessment model was the necessity to undertake a comprehensive system to skill-building staff development inservice training for school psychologists emphasizing consultative techniques, service-based psychological delivery models and sensitivity to multicultural factors impacting the need for service. Some of these programs were offered for continuing education college credit.

After all the components of the EMH reassessment had been completed, multidisciplinary staff conferences were held to make placement decisions. Considerable criticism was levelled at the evaluation process and the fact that sixty percent of the Black students in EMH were not removed, which was the suggestion of one of the lead consultants. Thirty percent were returned to the regular grades. Because the mandated timetable did not allow for intensive follow-up, additional study and analysis ensued. It should be borne in mind that classification or labelling did not drive the process; each student was looked upon as an individual who was deserving of concentrated personal attention. If the central concern was that of overrepresentation and the success of the project were to be dependent on the total number of students removed, a simple review of records and **reclassification** process could have occurred. Instead, an admittedly laborious and difficult program was undertaken that broke new ground in the reasons for, and uses of, assessment. It was pointed out that if, after developing a different approach for assessing the student, the same old research paradigms were used to evaluate the approach, it would not adequately respond to important issues of tapping the untapped potential of the individual.

There is much work to be done. Three important research proposals have been generated in order to investigate:

(a) the analysis of causal factors having significant being on the overrepresentation of Blacks in EMH,

(b) the link between the BCS Psychoeducation Procedures (now called Process Assessment for Learning) and the behavioral/ instructional objectives of the Chicago Public Schools.

(c) a neuropsychological/behavior assessment and intervention clinic to provide an accurate and indepth assessment of possible neuropsychological etiology of handicapped students and develop appropriate intervention programs.

All of the activities undertaken by the Bureau of Child Study in the last five years have had, as a central core, the desegregation focus of the entire school system and a desire to serve children equitably. The reinforcement and commendations received from many quarters have provided the impetus to continue without the resources available that would support such an effort. It was stated that :

"The Chicago experience is certainly one of the most important developments in the United States with respect to the urgent matter of devising more precise, equitable and helpful ways to identify and meet the special needs of school children. What you are doing is setting trends for much of the rest of the country."[16]

The Chicago experience with its past and present can offer lessons for the future.

---

[15]H. Carl Haywood OP CIT

The Detroit Public Schools' Experience with Alternatives to I.Q. Testing

by
Ingrid Draper, Aleatha Hamilton and Janet Jones

Special education in America has come full circle. As we examine the influences which have had significant impact upon the field, it becomes apparent that in our quest to work toward major special education reforms, new issues are now being raised that will require collaborative efforts between regular and special educators.

The decade of the 1960's raised the social, political and racial consciousness of the nation[1] and was followed in the 1970's by a period of litigation that established in the courts the constitutional rights of handicapped students to an education.[2] The decade of the 1970's also signaled a period of major legislative activity when the United States Congress enacted landmark special education laws; including Section 504 of the Rehabilitation Act and P.L. 94-142, The Education for All Handicapped Children Act, one of the most important pieces of civil rights legislation for the handicapped.[3]

With the complexity of major interrelated issues confronting educators throughout the country, the opportunity to bring about needed special education reforms; to re-examine historic and traditional special education practice in the light of expanded effective schools research that challenges traditional practice, is greater now than perhaps we have ever seen.[4]

The influences of litigation, legal mandates and the resulting impact upon special education practice has created a consciousness that makes it essential for special educators to take the lead in restructuring special education assessment, programs and services[5] and removing the barriers that

[1]Frederick J. Weintraub and Alan Abeson, "New Education Policies for the Handicapped: The Quiet Revolution," in Public Policy and the Education of Exceptional Children, ed. F.J. Weintraub, A. Abeson, J. Ballard and Martin LaVor (*The Council for Exceptional Children*, 1976).

[2]Barbara D. Bateman and Cynthia M. Herr, "Law and Special Education," in *Handbook of Special Education*, eds. James M. Kaufman and Daniel P. Hallahan (Englewood Cliffs, N.J.: Prentice-Hall, 1981).

[3]Lamar Mayer, *Educational Administration and Special Education: The Handbook for School Administrators* (Boston: Allyn and Baker, Inc., 1982).

[4]William E. Bickel and Donna D. Bickel, "Effective Schools, Classrooms and Instruction: Implications for Special Education," in *Exceptional Children*, vol. 52, no. 6 (1986), pp. 489-500; and Madeline C. Will, "Let Us Pause and Reflect - But Not Too Long," *Exceptional Children*, vol. 51, no. 1 (1984) pp. 11-16.

[5]Margaret C. Wang, Maynard C. Reynolds and Herbert J. Walberg, "Rethinking Special Education" *Educational Leadership* (1986).

have contributed to the development of a separate and compartmentalized delivery system.

With the implementation of P.L. 94-142, school systems are now providing educational opportunities to increasing numbers of severely impaired and multiply impaired students, a population that requires unique interdisciplinary and interagency collaborative support and services.[6] In addition, the impact on the broader community of normalization and de-institutionalization is resulting in fewer numbers of handicapped individuals in institutions and comparable increases in the number of persons residing in their homes and community settings and attending public school educational programs.

Many of the areas of educational practice that require reform in special education are not new. Other issues are emerging as educators prepare to effectively meet the needs of students not previously served in public schools and to re-examine the traditional, segregated, pull-out models so prevalent in the delivery system for mildly impaired students. It is apparent that large numbers of low-performing students do not fit either regular education or special education, but require collaborative efforts from the best that both programs have to offer.[7]

As the Detroit school system seeks to re-examine special education practice and to bring about needed reform from within special education, the following issues must be confronted within the context of system change:

1. Disproportionate numbers of Black students are referred and placed in special education programs on a national level,[8] with over 92% of the students in special education placed in classes for the mentally impaired, emotionally impaired, learning disabled and speech and language impaired.[9]
2. The system for determining special education eligibility is often inconsistent and non-specific.[10]
3. Multidisciplinary evaluation team decision-making practices must demonstrate the relationship of the categorical labels to improved

[6]Will, "Let Us Pause and Reflect - But Not Too Long."

[7]Wang, Reynolds and Walberg, "Rethinking Special Education."

[8]Kirby A. Heller, Wayne H. Holtzman and Samuel Messick, eds. *Placing Children in Special Education: A Strategy for Equity* (Washington, D.C.: National Academy Press, 1982).

[9]Bickel and Bickel, "Effective Schools, Classrooms and Instruction: Implications for Special Education."

[10]Gene V. Glass, "Effectiveness of Special Education," *Policy Studies Review*, vol. 2, special #1 (January, 1983); Want, Reynolds and Walberg, "Rethinking Special Education"; and James E. Ysseldyke; Bob A. Algozzine and J. Mitchell, "Special Education Decision Making: An Analysis of Current Practice," *Personnel and Guidance Journal*, vol. 60 (1982), pp. 308-313.

outcomes for students.[11] Interdisciplinary assessment practice must guide teaching and impact the effectiveness of educational intervention.[12]

4. More flexible special education services must be developed for mildly impaired students which remove the traditional barriers between regular education and special education and encourages integrated programming for students in less restricted settings.[13]

5. Interdisciplinary support and service to profoundly and severely handicapped students and interagency collaborative efforts must be developed to meet the unique needs of an increasingly impaired student population who often have multiple agency involvements outside of the school meeting.

6. Alternatives to current practice must be explored which focus upon the provision of improved services to students who are experiencing academic or adjustment difficulties in their local school setting without requiring a lengthy and expensive determination of special education eligibility process for all children before preventive and/or remedial support can be provided.

Efforts to bring about a climate for change within the Detroit system were developed in a planned, systematic and comprehensive manner and were consciously designed to touch all facets of the school system, including but not limited to, the district's chief school officers and decision makers, the Board of Education, general and special education administrators and teachers, counselors, psychologists, school social workers, teachers of the speech and language impaired, parents and community agencies.

Massive efforts were developed within the Office of Special Education, with the full support of the General Superintendent, Dr. Arthur Jefferson; and the Detroit Board of Education; the Executive Deputy Superintendent, Dr. Melvin Chapman; the Deputy Superintendent, Division of Educational Services, Dr. Stuart Rankin; and the seven Area Superintendents, over a four year period, to foster the climate for an introspective, objective look at information gathered to document the problems and to facilitate collaborative efforts on a system-wide basis to work toward change.

Some of the major collaborative activities that were undertaken included:

[11]Heller, Holtzman and Messick, eds. *Placing Children in Special Education: A Strategy for Equity.*

[12]James E. Ysseldyke and Mark R. Shinn, "Psychological Evaluation," in *Handbook of Special Education*, eds. J.M. Kaufman and D.P. Hallahan (Englewood Cliffs, N.J.: Prentice-Hall, 1981).

[13]Bickel and Bickel, "Effective Schools, Classrooms and Instruction: Implication for Special Education"; Wang, Reynolds and Walberg, "Rethinking Special Education"; and Will, "Let Us Pause and Reflect - But Not Too Long."

1. The development of system-wide procedural and operational guidelines for the district's multidisciplinary special education evaluation teams to foster consistency and to improve team functioning and communications.

   Product: Multidisciplinary Evaluation/Individualized Educational Planning Committee Guidelines for the Detroit Public Schools.

2. Mainstreaming guidelines were developed by a collaborative team of special education administrators and teachers, regular education administrators and teachers, and parent members of the Detroit Special Education Parent Advisory Committee. The guidelines provide information and strategies to central, area and local school staff and parents to assure full program access for handicapped students and consistency of mainstreaming practices at the local school level.

   Product: Mainstreaming Guidelines for the Detroit Public Schools.

3. The special education program review was a comprehensive yearlong review of the entire Detroit special education continuum of services with resulting recommendations focusing on program and service improvement activities. The effort, by design, was collaborative and involved special education administrators, principals, parents, community agency representatives, local, state and county staff.

   Product: Special Education Program Review and Recommendations.

4. The special education sex-equity plan was developed with a foundation of special education statistical information which documented the sex disproportion of black males in special education programs for the mentally impaired, emotionally impaired and the learning disabled.

   Product: Special Education Sex Equity Plan.

5. The special education component of the school district's strategic plan documents the focus of priority activities, recommended changes from traditional special education service models, strategies for expanded collaboration with regular education and major special education reform efforts targeted for a five year period.

   Product: Special Education Unit Strategic Plan.

6. A Parent Guide to Special Education Programs and Services provides basic information to parents and staff regarding the Education for All Handicapped Children Act and the Michigan Special Education Rules. The guide, developed collaboratively by parents and

staff, gives specific information about local special education policies that implement state and federal guidelines in the Detroit Public Schools. A description of the continuum of special education programs and services is also provided.

Product: A Parent Guide to Special Education Programs and Services in the Detroit Public Schools.

A massive inservice program was initiated by the Office of Special Education and funded by a grant from the United States Office of Education entitled: Detroit's Specialized Training Program for Chief School Officers. The aim of this project was to increase the knowledge, awareness and understanding of the district's chief decision makers of the federal and state rules that govern special education.

The inservice effort focused on the impact of the mandated special education laws and the recognition of the need for change in special education. While inservice was the goal of this three year activity, the development of increased staff awareness of the impact that aggressive implementation of P.L. 94-142 provisions was having on the special education system, in particular, and system practice, in general, was the key objective of all project activities.

The objectives of the Chief School Officers Project over the three year during cycle were:

YEAR ONE — 1983-1984 School Year

- To increase the knowledge of the legal mandates affecting the education of the handicapped.
- To increase knowledge of the impact of legislative implementation on regular and special education.

YEAR TWO — 1984-1985 School Year

- To increase knowledge of the eligibility standards for determining handicaps.
- To increase knowledge of the evaluation procedures for determining eligibility.
- To increase knowledge of the special education placement provisions.
- To increase knowledge of the impact of the eligibility standards and the evaluation procedures on regular and special education.

YEAR THREE — 1985-1986 School Year

- To increase knowledge of the impact of the eligibility standards and the evaluation procedures on regular and special education.
- To increase knowledge and understanding of the needs of special

regular education students and the resources available to assist and support their learning.

- To increase knowledge of the due process provisions of the mandated special education legislation.

The inservice project was established, planned and implemented in cooperation with the Office of Staff Development, Division of Human Resource Management and Development, and the Office of Special Education, Division of Educational Services. These inservice efforts were supported and shared by both divisions, offices and their staffs.

A central project planning team was assembled which consisted of representatives from each of the following services:

1. Curriculum and Achievement
2. Special Education Supervisory and Administrative Staff
3. School Social Work Service
4. School Psychology
5. School Community Relations

The planning team met together to identify specific tasks for the implementation of the project objectives and to identify District Area Teams which would replicate and implement the project in their respective Areas. In addition, the teams identified inservice dates, selected consultants and developed the process for achieving the project objectives which had been selected.

During each year, the inservice programs were presented to the highest level of the administrative staff of the district from the General Superintendent, the cabinet and executive staff, members of the Board of Education, Area Superintendents, Area staff and principals. The objectives were clear and the messages were replicated consistently to each group throughout the school year. The keynote speaker for the kick-off session was national acclaimed educator, Dr. Samuel Proctor, Professor of Urban Education at Rutgers University and Pastor of Abyssinian Baptist Church in New York City.

Cooperation and collaboration continued each year. A highlight of the second year was the production of a slide-tape presentation focusing on issues and procedures in evaluation, eligibility, and placement of children suspected as handicapped.

Over the life of Detroit's Specialized Training Program for Chief School Officers Project, the district's response to this effort was reflected in the questions and comments that were generated by the inservice programs. Year three activities were influenced largely by the change in awareness and attitudes that occurred during year one and two. Questions and issues raised by the Chief School Officers, area staff and principals helped to shape the direction of inservice activities and presentations for year three. The focus of the specific goals were redirected from this field-generated response to the knowledge imparted earlier. This event was viewed as most favorable since it represented a direct reflection of the success of the first two years of inservice.

These field-generated concerns spoke to issues such as: (1) improving the learning of low performing students as an alternative to special education placement; (2) addressing the needs and potential of the male child of African-American descent; (3) placement of handicapped students in regular education with support; (4) the identification and implementation of new and effective roles for special education teachers and evaluative staff; (5) strategies for serving the ineligible child in need of specialized intervention; and, (6) financing the necessary pre-referral intervention activities.

Dr. Asa Hilliard, Fuller E. Callaway Professor, Georgia State University, was contracted as chief project consultant for year three to specifically address the field-generated concerns. His expertise as a chief witness in court cases involving special education issues, as well as being a nationally known educator, psychologist and author, provided the district with knowledge, insight, enthusiasm and future possibilities for a professionally stimulating response to the inquiries of the district-wide target audience.

During these inservices with area staff, principals and other specially designated staff identified by the individual Area superintendents, audiences were given an opportunity to interact with the speaker through a variety of program formats.

The Chief School Officers Inservice project generated a new awareness in the school district regarding special education issues and concerns. Approximately 4,000 persons including administrators, staff, parents and community received inservice through this important project. As our district consciousness rose, a sense of urgency prevailed as we sought methods and additional strategies to address the pressing needs and issues that were being raised. For the first time, regular educators were challenged by knowing that the time was opportune for forming a true partnership with regular education in serving children with learning problems.

Seeing the vigorous effort to identify cooperative strategies and new skills to meet these educational needs, Dr. Hilliard introduced the theory, research and practice of Professor Reuven Feuerstein, the creator of Dynamic Assessment and Instrumental Enrichment.

Many of us had heard of the Instrumental Enrichment(I.E.) Program; however, few, if any of us, understood the undergirding theoretical assumptions of this program, or the clinically rigorous approach to dynamic assessment of low functioning individuals using the Learning Potential Assessment Device (L.P.A.D.). We soon learned that increased attention to Dynamic Assessment and I.E. was well deserved.

The L.P.A.D. and I.E. systems are designed to train deficient cognitive functions and encourages the identification of strategies that link the educator and evaluator in a relationship with children that focuses on the cognitive modifiability potential of the individual. These systems are viewed as dynamic and "open" because they are based on the premise that intelligence is not fixed but can be changed. The appropriate teaching of thinking and learning abilities afford the students an opportunity to increase their cognitive ability which leads to improved motivation, greater self-esteem and better school performance.

Certainly the Dynamic Assessment and Instrumental Enrichment System is not a panacea. One must remain constantly vigilant for other approaches that can serve this same function. However, we view this system as the most promising in support of structural change in special education and in stimulating broad-based reform. L.P.A.D. is not to be viewed as an instrument for determining special education eligibility and placement but rather a specialized set of tools that can be used effectively to design instructional interventions. This will include alternatives for low performing students who are not eligible for special education. As a result, we can raise our expectations that greater numbers of handicapped students can be returned to less restricted environments and to regular education with support.

Our reason for selecting Dynamic Assessment and Instrumental Enrichment is because the guiding philosophy and actual practice offers an assessment and instructional approach that is consistent with our reform goals. These systems assist in the creation of an assessment practice that has instructional utility. Our current evaluation practice is highly dependent on static, standardized intelligence and achievement measures that often do not result in the improvement of treatment practices. These traditional assessment approaches have been used as a means of classifying and excluding children from regular education and have fostered the development of a dual educational system; special and regular.

The National Research Council (U.S.) Panel on Selection and Placement of Students in Programs for the Mentally Retarded[14] highlights a major concern in this arena which is that the predictive power of the I.Q. test is insufficient evidence of the test's educational utility:

> "...However, the predictive power of the I.Q. does not necessarily make it a good measure of mental processes; different processes may underlie the same I.Q. scores for different groups of children, and different types of remediation may be necessary in cases

[14]Heller, Holtzman and Messick, *Placing Children in Special Education: A Strategy for Equity.*

of poor performance... Because of these and a host of other factors, there is no direct way to infer the source of the child's difficulty from incorrectly answered items, nor does a test score or profile of sub-scores provide the kind of information needed to design an individualized curriculum for a child in academic difficulty."[15]

We accept the premise that the main purpose of assessment in education is to improve instruction and learning. We believe that a significant number of children who experience learning difficulties can be treated with improved instruction; that assessment should identify strengths and weaknesses and assist in pinpointing the intervention and instruction necessary to remediate learning difficulties.

"A concern with instructional utility leads to a search for assessment procedures and instruments that will aid in selecting and designing effective programs for all children. We believe that better assessment and a closer link between assessment and instruction will, in fact, reduce disproportion, because minority children have disproportionately been the victims of poor instruction. We also believe that the problem should be attacked at its roots, which lie in the presumption that learning problems must imply deficiencies in the child and inconsequent inattention to the role of education itself in creating and ameliorating these problems."[16]

Thus, our search for new assessment procedures that are direct measures of learning must advance. The uniqueness of Feuerstein's L.P.A.D. is that it is directly linked to teaching and remedial instruction. Contrary to conventional measures which only assess what a child knows, Feuerstein puts the student in a situation in which there is something to learn and then observes how and what is learned.

The L.P.A.D. includes a wide variety of conceptual tasks involving analogies, seriation, logical classification, etc. Children are exposed to a highly structured instructional sequence involving explicitly verbal explanation (mediation) and practice and feedback usually in a one-to-one interaction with a trained teacher or evaluator. Children are then retested on the original tasks and on a set of related tasks designed to show how well newly learned concepts are generalized to similar problems. The child's potential is measured based on the degree of progress made in response to instruction.[17]

"The assumption guiding the development of the L.P.A.D. is not merely that the individual is active in registering, selecting, processing and communicating stimuli from both the external and internal environments — a defining characteristic of a paradigm adopted for much of modern psychology — but, rather, that the individual is an **open system** susceptible to influences which can produce **structural** changes in cognitive functioning. The dynamic assessment of learning potential targets the modifiability of the capacity to undergo such structural changes as a capacity which exists above and beyond any specific change or inculcation of skill. Conceptualizing and dealing very specifically with the process of change, the L.P.A.D. neither produces an inventory of what the

[15]Ibid., p. 19.
[16]Ibid., p. 72.
[17]Ibid., P. 60-61.

examiner knows, nor produces a stable product such as an intelligence quotient. The L.P.A.D., rather, seeks to identify the causes which prevent the examinee from functioning at higher levels and, through an assessment of the learner's modifiability, to produce information about the type, amount and nature of investments which may be required to move, bypass or overcome these obstacles and permit the examinee to accede to higher levels of functioning."[17]

The L.P.A.D. is one of the most promising practices for examining and remediating the cognitive functioning of individuals. The Instrumental Enrichment Program, L.P.A.D.'s instructional companion, provides a structured step-by-step mediated learning experience. The I.E. Program can be used prescriptively, or as a whole class intervention to modify cognitive abilities. The system is a true example of testing, serving instruction.

The testament to the impact of these systems is the reception that they receive from Detroit teachers and evaluative staff who have become involved in our pilot effort. In every school where Instrumental Enrichment instruction takes place, we witness enthusiasm expressed on the part of staff and students regarding its effect and influence in creating teacher and student change. During the L.P.A.D. training and demonstration sessions, evaluators and teachers express appreciation for systems that do not merely rank and confirm low functioning but rather seek ways to change low levels of performance. One of our greatest challenges has been dealing with the disappointment of staff who are **not** involved in our initial pilot effort.

Our involvement with Dynamic Assessment began in December, 1985, with a training session conducted by Dr. Asa Hilliard. The initial group trained included twenty interdisciplinary staff members comprised of special education teacher consultants, teachers of the speech and language impaired, school social workers, school psychologists and supervisors. The group also included one special education teacher. (Currently, the group has expanded to include a total of forty members.) Although the training group was limited, the audit audience consisted of parents, regular educators, (including Chapter 1 and bilingual education representatives), administrative, county and state level participants. In addition, we were so impressed by the promise of the program, that avenues were pursued to secure the most extensive training available. The school district at that time was not prepared to support a trip to Jerusalem to study under Dr. Feuerstein; however, an influential letter was sent to Dr. Feuerstein inviting him to Detroit to train our staff.

---

[18]Mogens R. Jensen and Reuven Feuerstein, The Dymanic Assessment of Retarded Performers with the Learning Potential Assessment Device: From Philosophy to Practice. To appear in Dynamic Assessment: Foundations and Fundamentals, ed. C. Lidz (New York, N.Y.: Guilford Press - currently in press).

In the meantime, we knew that the local source of Dynamic Assessment training in this country was available from Dr. Mogens Jensen of Yale University. Therefore, the district supported the travel of a select interdisciplinary team of nine persons to participate in an L.P.A.D. workshop conducted by Dr. Jensen at Columbia University Teachers' College in New York City in the spring of 1986.

This cadre of individuals exposed to the advanced training and experience provided by Drs. Hilliard and Jensen formed a network of commitment and assisted in suggesting and implementing both formal and informal activities designed to prepare the path for L.P.A.D. in Detroit. These strategies included the following:

1. Awareness presentations were conducted by the members of the Advance Team to their respective departments. (Teacher Consultants, Teachers of the Speech and Language Impaired, School Social work, School Psychology)
2. Periodic support meetings were held with the Advance Team members in order to update them on the progress of the project, to disseminate additional information and to share experiences related to L.P.A.D. practice.
3. A special one day inservice led by Dr. Hilliard was conducted with each of the major groups working inside the special education delivery system. (Special Education Teachers, Special Education Teacher Consultants, Teachers of the Speech and Language Impaired, School Social Workers, School Psychologists and Supervisors and Administrators)
4. A special meeting was held with the General Superintendent, the Executive Deputy Superintendent, the Deputy Superintendent and the Area Superintendents to present information and to increase the awareness of the project goals.
5. A special presentation was made by members of the advance team at a committee meeting of the Detroit Board of Education to explain Dymanic Assessment and the results of the training effort.

The 1985-86 school year culminated with a special Summer Institute sponsored by the Office of Special Education that received broad based participation in the planning and implementation. The Institute's title was "Student Achievement: Visions Beyond the Possible." Approximately 500 participants representing primarily special educators but including regular educators, parents and community persons attended the fifty workshop offerings that emphasized the development of specialized instructional strategies and pedagogy to improve assessment and instruction. The highlight of the Institute was the Dynamic Assessment training conducted by Dr. Reuven Feuerstein, assisted by Dr. Kevin Keane, Consultant, Columbia Teachers' College and Dr. Asa Hilliard. The Instrumental Enrichment Training for thirty special education teachers was conducted by Ms. Frances Link of Curriculum Development Associates, Washington, D.C.; also held during the Summer Institute. Dr. Hilliard remained throughout the Institute and served as a keynote speaker and conducted specialized workshops for select interest groups on the philosophy and potential impact of Dynamic Assessment on student learning.

Participation in the workshop session was entirely voluntary. Our observations and a review of the workshop evaluations confirm for us that there are significant numbers of staff who are motivated and willing to seek professional answers to difficult problems in education on their own time, if given the opportunity.

The success of our project thus far has been dependent on several key factors that will have significant impact in most situations and are itemized herein:

1. The leadership of the Office of Special Education held a steadfast commitment to significantly change special education from within. This attitude was influential in many ways. **First**, support was given by Dr. Stuart Rankin, Deputy Superintendent of the Division of Educational Services, who holds administrative responsibility for special education, pupil personnel services and curriculum in the school district. **Second**, the priorities of the Office of Special Education expanded to include a major focus on change and reform. As special education supervisory staff became actively involved in the project, they were reinforced by learning the theory of Structural Cognitive Modifiability and ''open'' systems approaches to assessment and instruction. The need for change became a common achievable goal and commitment. Special education supervisors and administrators actively participated in the training and formed a strong, internal support network for the project.

2. The L.P.A.D. trainees were selected with an interdisciplinary focus and spirit, including special education teacher consultants, school psychologists, teachers of speech and language and school social workers. Every effort was made to increase the awareness of all groups involved in the special education delivery system. This approach fostered the teaming between disciplines. Certainly, some disciplines will use the L.P.A.D. more extensively than others; while other disciplines will incorporate the theory and select components of the practice as part of their repertoire of competencies within their

disciplines. The use of L.P.A.D. is not restricted to any one discipline. The decision to use Dynamic Assessment will be based on the student's need and the L.P.A.D. practitioners will be those persons designated by the school district as being thoroughly trained and prepared to use it to the benefit of the instructional process.

3. On-going systematic efforts to keep keypersons and groups involved and aware of the project was paramount:

   — on-going communication with the Deputy Superintendent, and the Executive Deputy Superintendent, and the General Superintendent

   — planned presentations to the Secondary, Adult, Special Education Committee of the Detroit Board of Education

   — presentations and training opportunities were provided to parents and community with the involvement and participation of the Detroit Special Education Parent Advisory Group

   — invitations and opportunities were extended to regular instructional and administrative staff to participate in the training workshops

   — structured activities to promote awareness among key county, state and university personnel were provided

   — direct involvement and opportunities were provided to the supervisory and administrative staff from school psychology, school social work and special education in the selection of the L.P.A.D. trainees and in the actual L.P.A.D. training workshops

4. Regular support meetings were held for the members of the Advance L.P.A.D. group in order to consistently share new information, ideas and problems. These meetings were instrumental in developing a sense of family and comraderie among L.P.A.D. examiners. Additionally, a concerted effort was made to ensure that there was a match with the school assignments, the L.P.A.D. examiners and the schools implementing the Instrumental Enrichment program in special education classes. This was not only a criteria for staff selection, but a practical way to form meaningful and influential support groups at the building level.

Currently the Detroit project encompasses forty L.P.A.D. trainees and forty-nine I.E. teachers attached to twenty-seven project schools. The I.E. program is being used with various special education populations including the Learning Disabled, the Educable Mentally Impaired, the Emotionally Impaired, the Hearing Impaired, the Visually Impaired and the Trainable Mentally Impaired.

Regular inservice and support meetings are held with the Instrumental Enrichment teachers and the principals of the pilot schools. This type of organized staff development is essential to build and develop the skills necessary to implement the program.

The establishment of a Mediated Learning Experience Center which serves as a center for study, research and practice. This Center is another source for staff development as the project expands.

5. Systematic efforts were made to document the project vis-a-vis video taping and photo documentaries. This became an excellent way to capture the significant milestones and major activities for use in future training sessions.

School districts desiring to implement Dynamic Assessment practice will encounter significant problems. Some problems can be handled through creative and aggressive management, whereas other issues must be addressed through a dramatic shift in public policies and practices. Major issues include the following:

1. The L.P.A.D. examiner must have a thorough knowledge of the L.P.A.D. tools, the cognitive map, the deficient functions and the mental operations as well as acquire skill as a mediator. **The very nature of Dynamic Assessment dictates that the instrument of assessment is the assessor, not the L.P.A.D. tools.** Therefore, acquiring expert training and supervised practice is a critical component. The minimum training period is two (2) five day workshop segments usually delivered within a two-three month period of time. This must be accompanied with intensive practice and followed by periodic supervision.

Additionally, the L.P.A.D. examiner should also receive training in the use of Instrumental Enrichment to be fully effective. This means that sufficient funds must be made available to train the staff and to purchase materials. Also, the select staff must be freed of on-going responsibility to participate in the training and practice on a periodic basis.

Another consequence is that a substantial effort must be made to ensure the development of an internal capacity to train others. This will generate independence from expensive and oftentimes inaccessible consultants and trainers.

2. The L.P.A.D./I.E. approach requires a change in the attitudes of all person involved. The traditional way of thinking about education is burdened with the existence of ranking and labeling practices.

However, the question remains whether the label has any educational relevance. The labels lead to assumptions that these students cannot be served in regular education. Thus, "pull-out" approaches are created. "Although well-intentioned, this so-called 'pull-out' approach to the educational difficulties of students with learning problems has failed in many instances to meet the educational needs of these students and has created, however unwittingly, barriers to successful education."[18]

This highlights the critical need to educate the public and educational community to the goals and benefits of an alternative "open" systems approach such as Dynamic Assessment. Also, there must be organized efforts to involve and to elicit the support of persons at the county, state and federal levels as projects of a similar nature are developed. It is important that all persons involved have increased opportunities to learn how this system is amenable to the unification of services for low performing students and how this system has as its main purpose the improvement of instruction.

3. School districts must create a receptive environment for the work of the L.P.A.D. examiner. Serious attention must be given to supporting the staff persons who are preparing themselves as L.P.A.D. examiners. Persons who are involved in the process need district support as they attempt to work together to change historic evaluation practice. The L.P.A.D. examiner may experience some ambivalence if there are too few opportunities afforded to practice the new skills. Extraordinary efforts must be developed to ensure broad based communication and involvement as project activities are developed and implemented so that criticism from persons unfamiliar with the project goals will be minimized.

Interdisciplinary support networks are essential to maintain communication and opportunities for teaming.

One suggestion is to organize interdisciplinary support networks at the school as well as the district level. For example, matching the L.P.A.D. examiners with schools using the I.E. program will facilitate collaborative and support activities involving the principal and the regular and special teachers in the school.

An agenda of periodic support groups' meetings and continual inservice must be fostered. A Center for study and practice should be

---

[19]Will, "Let Us Pause and Reflect - But Not Too Long," p. 412.

established within the district. Concerted efforts should be made to form a national network of support among school districts as the work in this area grows.

It must be emphasized that Dynamic Assessment is but one avenue to our goal. The search for like systems that advocate and generate the ''open system'' viewpoint of assessment and instruction as exemplified by Dynamic Assessment is continual. Our goal is to focus on the development of those skills and attitudes that maximize the opportunity for assessment to serve instruction.

We look forward to the continuing challenges and opportunities to chart a different course for special education - to maintain the practices that are educationally effective and result in higher achievement levels for our students and to discard some of the traditional practices that have not served our students well. The future will bring expanded collaborative activities to:

— Develop more flexible models of service delivery for mildly impaired handicapped students in less restricted programs.

— Ensure greater collaboration and teaming between special educators and general educators that meet the needs of low performing students who may not qualify for special education but who are the very students who are over-referred for evaluation and special education placement.

— Examine alternative referral, assessment, intervention and local school support models that improve services to students and their teachers.

— Explore and develop more effective interdisciplinary and inter-agency collaborative models that effectively meet the needs of severely impaired and multiple impaired students and their families.

— Examine current assessment practice and procedures and restructure, within current legal constraints, to enable more opportunities for interdisciplinary support staff to increase direct intervention and consultation services to students and teachers.

— Examine the current funding policies on a state and national level which may well be barriers to the delivery of services to many low performing students who do not 'fit' the special education eligibility guidelines but who require specialized intervention services.

The challenges ahead for special education are great - but we can and must meet those challenges directly and seize the opportunity to reexamine current special education assessment and program practice in the context of system change. Without question, special education practice must change.

The future is bright for improved collaborations and teaming among general education and special education staff and parents as educational services and local school support systems are improved for **all** children.

Court Bans Use of I.Q. Tests For Blacks For Any Purpose In California State Schools: Press Release by Law Offices of Public Advocates, Inc., San Francisco, California

by

H.E. Dent, A.M. Mendocal, W.D. Pierce and G.I. West

Federal District Judge Robert F. Peckham, Chief Judge of Northern California, signed an order on September 25, 1986, approving an agreement between the California State Department of Education (SDE) and the plaintiffs in the **Larry P.** case. This agreement provides for the court to issue an order directing the SDE to notify all California school districts that standardized individual tests of intelligence (I.Q. tests) can no longer be administered to Black students **for any purpose**.

This settlement culminates fifteen years of legal action which officially began on November 24, 1971, when Black parents in San Francisco filed a class action suit on behalf of their children who had been inappropriately placed in Educable Mentally Retarded (EMR) special education classes. The parents were supported by members of the Bay Area Association of Black Psychologists who had tested these children and found that the children were not mentally retarded and should not have been placed in special education classes.

The new court order directs the Superintendent of Public Instruction to send a directive to all California school districts informing them that there is now "a complete prohibition against using I.Q. tests for identifying or placing Black pupils in special education." For the past ten years, the State Department of Education and school districts have devised various pretenses for getting around the previous court orders banning I.Q. testing. For example, the SDE told districts that I.Q. tests could be used with parental consent or "to develop a pupils strengths and weaknesses." Judge Peckham's new order goes through each of those excuses for continued testing and says that each is "not a permissible justification for the administration of an I.Q. test to a Black pupil." Further, the new order directs the SDE to review the districts' records to assure compliance with the directive on I.Q. testing. A copy of the order is enclosed.

Dr. Gerald West, a professor at San Francisco State University and a witness who testified at trial, stated that "The **Larry P.** case is significant because it is the first successfully litigated case disproving theories of racial intellectual inferiority." William Pierce, also a trial expert witness, added

165

that the order is "a long but necessary first step to the fair psychological assessment of Black Americans."

The suit was brought because, until now, school officials throughout the State had relied upon I.Q. test results to label many normal Black children as mentally retarded or learning disabled. In the State of California, approximately nine percent of the children in the public schools are Black, yet twenty-five percent of the students in classes for the mentally retarded were Black. The consequences of this misplacement has been devastating, setting back a child's education, and destroying a child's self image and sense of worth.

In its original judgment on December 12, 1979, the Federal District Court found that I.Q. tests were culturally biased against Black children because they do not account for the cultural background and experiences of Black people, have not been validated for the purpose for which they were being used, and, resulted in the disproportionate representation of Black children in special education classes. The Judge banned the use of I.Q. tests on Black children in the State of California for the purpose of placing those students in classes for the educable mentally retarded or classes serving substantially the same functions. The EMR program officially ceased as a separate categorized program after 1982, but almost all districts continue to place students who are identified as mildly mentally retarded into separate, self-contained classes, just as occurred in the EMR program.

The SDE appealed the December 12, 1979 decision and on June 25, 1986, the U.S. Court of Appeals for the Ninth Circuit affirmed the District Court's judgment opening the door for the negotiations that resulted in the agreement approved by Judge Peckham on September 25, 1986.

School districts will now have to employ other means for determining the educational needs of Black students. According to the settlement, the SDE is required to monitor the special education placement rates by race and ethnicity for the next three years to insure compliance by local school districts.

This lawsuit was filed by attorneys from Public Advocates, Inc., San Francisco Neighborhood Legal Assistance Foundation, California Rural Legal Assistance, and the NAACP Legal Defense Fund on behalf of all Black school children in California who have been, or may in the future, be wrongly classified.

In the six month trial in 1977-78, and appeal, the class of all Black children in EMR have been represented by Public Advocates, Inc. and Morrison and Foerster.

A detailed fact sheet, prepared by Dr. Harold Dent for the Bay Area Association of Black Psychologists, is enclosed.

A Fact Sheet

THE LARRY P. CASE

1. The **Larry P.** case is a class action suit brought by a group of Black parents in San Francisco whose children had been inappropriately classified and placed in classes for the Educable Mentally Retarded (EMR) in the San Francisco Unified School District.

2. The suit was filed in the U.S. District Court for the Northern District of California on November 24, 1971 (No. C-71-2270 FRP), naming as defendants the California State Superintendent of Public Instruction, the members of the California State Board of Education, the Superintendent of Schools for the San Francisco Unified School District and the members of the San Francisco Board of Education.

3. The suit contended that the civil rights of the children, guaranteed by the Fourteenth Amendment of the Constitution, had been violated and they had been denied equal opportunity to education guaranteed by the Civil Rights Act of 1964 and the California Education Code.

4. The plaintiffs alleged:

   A. That their children had been inappropriately classified and placed in EMR classes;

   B. That their children represent a class of "all Black children in the state wrongfully labelled and retained in EMR classes";

   C. That the plaintiffs' children and the class they represent had never been mentally retarded but had been wrongfully placed in EMR classes by reason of utilization by school districts throughout the state of standardized I.Q. tests which fail to account for their (plaintiffs' children) cultural background and home experiences;

   D. That testing procedures are authorized and required by the California State Department of Education;

   E. That pursuant to the California Education Code (section 6902), such classes should be designed to make EMR students "economically useful and socially adjusted."

5. The use of culturally biased I.Q. tests resulted in a disproportionately large number of Black children being wrongly labelled mentally retarded and inappropriately placed in EMR classes.

   For example: In 1969, 28.5% of the students enrolled in the San Francisco Unified School District were Black, but 58% of the students in EMR classes in San Francisco were Black. In the same year, 9.1% of all students in public schools in the State of California were Black, but 27.5% of all students in EMR classes in the state were Black.

6. The data for state enrollment in 1973 were essentially the same as they were in 1969, 9% of the public school students were Black, 25% of those in EMR classes were Black. However, actual numbers of students in EMR classes in the state had decreased markedly, from almost 55,000 in 1969 to 34,000 in 1973. The proportions remained the same.

7. At the other end of the continuum there was a disproportionately small number of Black children enrolled in the classes for Mentally Gifted Minors (MGM). In 1969 the State Department of Education reported only 2.5% of the children in MGM classes were Black, yet 9% of the children in public schools were Black.

8. On June 21st, 1972, Judge Robert F. Peckham issued a preliminary injunction against the San Francisco Unified School District to enjoin the district from requiring the use of I.Q. tests that do not account for the cultural and experiential background of Black children.

9. The San Francisco Unified School District appealed that injunction. In August 1973 the Ninth Circuit Court of Appeals upheld Peckham's decision.

10. The plaintiffs went back to court and asked Judge Peckham to extend his injunction to the State of California on behalf of all Black children inappropriately placed in EMR classes.

11. On December 14th, 1974, Judge Peckham extended the class of children to include all Black children in the State of California (inappropriately classified EMR) and enjoined the state from requiring the use of culturally biased I.Q. tests for the purpose of placing Black children in EMR classes.

12. At its December 1974 meeting, the California State Board of Education declared a moratorium on the use of I.Q. tests on **all** children being considered for EMR placement.

13. The Larry P. trial began October 11th, 1977 and final arguments were heard on May 30th, 1978. Among the witnesses for the plaintiffs were ABPsi members: Asa Hilliard, Ed.D., Reginald Jones, Ph.D., Gerald West, Ph.D., William Pierce, Ph.D., and Harold Dent, Ph.D. Other expert witnesses called by the plaintiffs included: Gloria Powell, M.D., Alice Watkins, Ph.D., Jane Mercer, Ph.D., George Albee, Ph.D., and Leon Kamin, Ph.D.

14. Defense witnesses included: Lloyd Humphreys, Ph.D., Nadine Lambert, Ph.D., Robert Thorndike, Ph.D., Leo Munday, Ph.D., and Jerome Doppelt, Ph.D.

15. Almost a year and half after closing arguments, October 16, 1979, Judge Peckham issued his landmark decision (No. C-71-2270 RFP). The Court found:

   A. That Federal and State Constitutional law and federal statutory law and been violated. (The Civil Rights Act of 1964, Section 504 of the Rehabilitation Act of 1973 and the Education for all Handicapped Children's Act of 1975.);

   B. That I.Q. tests were culturally biased and had not been validated for the purpose for which they were being used, placement of Black children in EMR classes;

   C. That the plaintiff's constitutional rights to equal education had been violated by wrongfully confining them to "dead end" EMR classes;

   D. That the plaintiffs' constitutional guarantees of equal protection by the laws had been violated by the State's "... unjustified toleration of disproportionate enrollments of Black children in EMR classes, and the use of placement mechanisms, particularly I.Q. tests, that perpetuate those disproportions..." (p.3);

   E. That "Defendants' conduct, in connection with the history of I.Q. testing and special education in California, reveals an unlawful segregative intent. This intent was not necessarily to hurt Black children, but it was an intent to assign a grossly disproportionate number of Black children to the special EMR classes, and it was manifested, **inter alia**, in the use of invalidated and racially and culturally biased placement criteria." (p. 3 and 4).

16. The Court ordered the following injunctive relief:

   A. "Defendants are enjoined from utilizing, permitting the use of, or approving the use of any standardized intelligence test... for the identification of Black EMR children or their placement into EMR classes, without securing approval of the Court." (p. 104).

   B. "Defendants are hereby ordered to monitor and eliminate disproportionate placement of Black children in California's EMR classes." (p.105).

C. "To remedy the harm to Black children who have been misidentified as EMR pupils and to prevent these discriminatory practices from recurring in California with respect to a similarly situated class of youngsters in the future, the defendants shall direct each school district to reevaluate every Black child currently identified as an EMR pupil without including in the psychological evaluation a standardized intelligence or ability test, that has not been approved by the court..." (p. 106-107).

17. In December 1979 the California State Board of Education voted **not** to appeal the Larry P. decision.

18. Wilson Riles, then State Superintendent of Public Instruction, **did** appeal the Larry P. decision.

19. On January 23rd, 1984 the U.S. Court of Appeals for the Ninth Circuit affirmed the district court's findings of violation of federal statutes, but found it unnecessary to reach federal constitutional issues. The appellate court also affirmed the finding of violation of California's constitutional equal protection provision.

20. the State Department of Education filed a petition for rehearing **en banc** (Rehearing by the entire bench; that is, a rehearing by all 29 judges of the Appellate Court.)

21. On June 25th, 1986, the Appellate Court issued an amended decision which:

   A. Denied the petition for rehearing;

   B. Rejected the motion for an **en banc** review;

   C. Reaffirmed the district court findings of violation of federal statutory law and the required remedy;

   D. Reversed the finding of violations of federal and state constitutional law.

Harold E. Dent, Ph.D.
Bay Area Association of Black Psychologists
August 1986

| LARRY P., by his Guardian ad litem, LUCILLE P., et al.,

Plaintiffs

v.

WILSON RILES, Superintendent of Public Instruction for the State of California, et al.,

Defendants. |)
)
)
)
)
)
)
)
)
)
)
)
)
)
) | NO. C-71-2770 RFP

**ORDER MODIFYING
JUDGMENT** |

On December 12, 1979, the Court entered its judgment in the above-entitled action. On June 25, 1986, the judgment of the district court was affirmed in part and reversed in part by the Court of Appeals.

On September 11, 1986, a Stipulated Request for Modification of Judgment was filed. On September 16, 1986, a hearing was held to consider the request for modification. This Court is satisfied that good cause exists for modification of the judgment as set forth in the Stipulation. Accordingly, it is hereby ordered that this Court's judgment of December 12, 1979 is modified in the following respects:

Data Collecting, Reporting and Monitoring

1. As part of the April pupil count, the defendant State Department of Education ("SDE") now collects data on all special classes by ethnicity, including the number of mentally retarded pupils in special day classes. The forms and instructions for the 1986 April pupil count are attached to the stipulation on file as Exhibit A. The Department will collect enrollment data for mentally retarded pupils by ethnicity and by type of class placement for the school years 1985-86, 1986-87, and 1987-88.

2. SDE will compare the enrollment of Black mentally retarded pupils in special day classes in each district to determine whether possible over-representation exists according to the "E" formula. Information regarding possible over-representation shall be forwarded to the consultants responsible for reviewing school districts as part of the SDE's Coordinated Compliance

Monitoring Review ("CCR") process. Districts found to have apparent disproportionate enrollments must explain the disproportionate enrollments, and, if necessary, develop a corrective action plan. The SDE reviewer must follow up on the district's plan, and the district's assessment procedures must be carefully reviewed for compliance with law and the SDE's directive on I.Q. testing, discussed **infra**. at paragraph 6.

3. The SDE shall provide plaintiffs' counsel with the enrollment data as set forth in paragraph one for the school years 1985-86, upon request, a reasonable opportunity to inspect and copy the CCR reports of the district reviewed in those years.

4. Within 60 days after receipt of the 1987-88 enrollment data, plaintiffs must either file with the Court a motion for contempt or further injunctive relief because of alleged non-compliance or the SDE's obligation to report data and to report monitoring results except as provided in paragraph 5, shall cease.

5. If the SDE continues to maintain a process for data collecting and monitoring (whether called CCR or not) beyond two more years, it will contain each of the following elements: (a) districts will annually report the enrollment of mentally retarded pupils separately for each ethnicity and race in special day classes; (b) the SDE will identify districts with apparent disproportionate enrollments of mentally retarded Black pupils in special day classes; (c) on-site reviews will investigate and, where appropriate, require corrective action (see, e.g., CCR Manual S.5e); and (d) on-site reviews will investigate all districts to assure that violations do not occur of the SDE's directive prohibiting I.Q. tests in the assessment of Black pupils who have been referred for special education services (see, e.g., CCR Manual S.5f). This obligation shall not be construed to create an independent commitment by the SDE to continue the CCR process in the future.

I.Q. Testing

6. Within 30 days of the filing of this order modifying the judgment, the SDE shall send the following directive on I.Q. testing from the Superintendent of Public Instruction to all California school districts and all SELPA directors:

"The purpose of this notice is to clarify the proper use of I.Q. tests in the assessment of Black pupils for special education services.

"School districts are not to use intelligence tests in the assessment of Black pupils who have been referred for special education services.

"In lieu of I.Q. tests, districts should use alternative means of assessment to determine identification and placement. Such techniques should include, and would not be limited to, assessment of pupil's personal history and development, adaptive behavior, classroom performance, academic achievement, and evaluative instruments designed to point out specific information relative to a pupil's abilities and inabilities in specific skill areas.

"The complete prohibition against using I.Q. tests for identifying or placing Black pupils in special education means that parents of Black pupils shall not be asked if they want to consent to the use of such tests. An I.Q. test may not be given to a Black pupil even with parental consent. Moreover, when a school district receives records containing test protocols from other agencies such as regional centers, out-of-state school districts, military facilities, or independent assessors, these records shall be forwarded to the parent. I.Q. scores contained in the records shall not become a part of the pupil's current school record.

"There are no special education related purposed for which I.Q. tests shall be administered to Black pupils. The following reasons are **not** permissible justifications for the administration of an I.Q. test to a Black pupil:

1) As part of a comprehensive educational plan to which a parent has consented;

2) To gain diagnostic information;

3) To develop goals and objectives;

4) To determine a special education pupil's educational needs; or

5) To develop a pupil's strengths and weaknesses as elicited by the I.Q. test.

"Further, an I.Q. test has been determined to be invalid with regard to Black pupils in assessments for specific learning disabilities. Thus, an I.Q. test may not be utilized for specific learning disability assessment purposes.

"The Department is aware that districts do not place or identify pupils on the basis of only I.Q. scores. However, the prohibition on I.Q. tests goes further and prohibits **any** use of an I.Q. test as part of an assessment which could lead to special education placement or services, even if the test is only part of a comprehensive assessment plan.

"The prohibition on I.Q. testing applies even though pupils are no longer placed in special 'day classes designated as 'E.M.R.'

"This directive supercedes all previous notices as to the meaning and effect of the Court's decision in **Larry P.** v. **Riles**. Specifically, the following previous statements, guidelines, or interpretations are superceded by this directive:

"Department Policy on the use of I.Q. Tests", SDE-OSE, July 10, 1979, Gordon Duck; "Implementation of 'Larry P.' Court Decision, Robert W. Garten, August 20, 1980; "Assessment - Certain Tests for Pupils Who May be Mentally Retarded: PSU Policy Research Paper, 4/11/82; Letter, Betty Hanson and Gerald Miller to Irv Sobel and Al Casler, August 27, 1982; "A Manuel for the Determination of a Severe Discrepancy as Defined by Title 5, CAC, Section 3030(j)", SDE-OSE, 1983; "Guidelines for Reviewing the Use of I.Q. Tests", SDE Service Assurance/Compliance Unit, September 11, 1985.

"A review of district's use of I.Q. tests in compliance with this directive shall be part of the Coordinated Compliance Monitoring Review process."

7. The following sections of the CCR Manual which concern the use of I.Q. test shall be modified to reflect the prohibition on I.Q. testing of Black pupils: S.3c; S.3e-6; S.31; 3.5f.

8. Except as set forth above, or insofar as the judgment was reversed by the Court of Appeal, all other provisions of the judgment of December 12, 1979, remain unmodified.

DATED: September 25, 1986

HONORABLE ROBERT F.
PECKHAM
Judge, U.S. District Court

Approved.
DATED: September 23, 19986

ARMANDO M. MENOCAL, III
Public Advocates, Inc.

SAMUAL R. MILLER
Morrison & Foerster

By _____
Attorneys for Plaintiffs

Approved.
DATED: September 18,1986

CHARLTON G. HOLLAND
Assistant Attorney General
ASHER RUBIN
Deputy Attorney General

By _____
Attorneys for Defendants

C-71-2770 RFP   LARRY P., by his Guardian ad litem, LUCILLE P., et al, vs. WILSON RILES, Superintendent of Public Instruction for the State of California, et al.

The Learning Potential Assessment Device and Instrumental Enrichment as a Paradigm Shift

by
Asa G. Hilliard, III

Reuven Feuerstein's LPAD/IE system is a novel contribution to the field of measurement and education. Both the LPAD and IE not only aim at the destruction of predictive validity as we have known it, they will challenge as well the fixation on the **function of prediction in pedagogy**. Once the static nature of traditional status assessment has been challenged successfully, a real new beginning will be possible for testing to serve instruction. It is not only the traditional I.Q. instruments, but the entire conceptual apparatus which supports the use of such instruments which either must be reconstructed or abandoned altogether.

Feuerstein's contribution represents a fresh start. Not only is the concept of modifiability 180 degrees away from traditional stasis assessment, Feuerstein has given us one of the few and perhaps the only valid approach to date, which moves from constructs, to pedagogical theory, to instruments, and to remedial strategies. The differences between the LPAD/IE system and traditional I.Q. based assessment are so great, that once the differences are understood generally, fundamental changes will be forced in the practice of educational psychology. Although the fact that some of the instruments which are utilized in the LPAD/IE, such as the **Raven's coloured progressive matrices** type problem, may appear to be the same, or even in some cases, identical to some older testing instruments, Feuerstein's **use** of those instruments is revolutionary.

The decision to attempt to understand problem solving dynamics and the belief that it is possible to intervene to shape that process, along with the demonstrated success in doing just that by skilled users of both **LPAD** and **ID,** should result ultimately in wholesale positive changes in professional practice.

Having attended workshops led by Feuerstein and his associates at Yale University, and having observed both **IE** and the **LPAD** in practice; and having worked directly with a number of children using the materials, there is one thing which has continued to impress me. Students become quickly and enthusiastically engaged in LPAD/IE activities. Over and over again, I have seen students who were labeled retarded, or who some professionals had thought might be retarded, come to life as they experience the power of learning prestigious, complex and difficult tasks. Their self-image and self-esteem is transformed in a very short period of time as their achievement increases.

In my own work with Dr. Grace Massey and the late Dr. Jean Carew in 1981, we were interested in "normal" departures from the "norm" in the measurement of toddlers who were taking the Bayley developmental scales showed clearly that a simple global score was really a stasis score which masked many significant things. For example, we observed a group of toddlers who we chose to describe as "creative," as contrasted with another group of more conforming children who we classified as traditional. The conforming acquiescent children had the highest scores. However, the video taped protocols showed the creative group tended to follow their own agenda. They were less willing to "play-the-game" but did not appear to us to be less able. In fact, they appeared to be much more able than the other groups. They simply got no credit for some of the complex, novel and unexpected things which they did, nor could we rule out their ability to do the "failed" tasks that they were clearly just **unwilling** to do.

Clearly, there is much more to respondent behavior than traditional assessment can reveal. Consequently, we should expect traditional assessment error of major proportion in both any description of present level of functioning and in judgments derived from testing to assist in the design of valid instruction.

A word must also be said about traditional options among instructional "treatments." Since the goal of traditional assessment is to predict **future** performance in order to assign students to differentiated "appropriate" pedagogical treatments or methods, such treatments must exist in fact if the predictive model is to work. Although many teaching strategies are presented in professional education course-work, and although some may be valid, there is no such thing as an accepted "standard procedure" for teaching the gifted, average, or retarded learners. We may best describe the existing situation as methodological anarchy. The pros and cons of such a situation need not be debated here, unless the value or validity of the extant traditional assessment system is questioned. What possible pedagogical utility could there be for an assessment system which is based on **prediction** and **categorical labeling**, when the presumption of a differentiated pedagogy cannot be substantiated? Empirical observations of gifted, average, and retarded classes will not reveal common practices differentiated by category, let along valid categorical practices.

Many educators are no strangers to the fact that skilled teaching can help low achieving students to make great leaps in academic performance. It happens everyday in public and private schools throughout the nation! The Marcus Garvey Elementary School in Los Angeles, the Dunbar Elementary School in Atlanta, The Pease Elementary School in Austin, Texas, the Oakland Community School in Oakland, California, the Nairobi Day School in East Palo Alto, California, are but a few of the schools which have a long and solid track record of student academic achievement, as measured in traditional terms. For years, success stories such as these have been regarded by professionals as isolated anomalies, if indeed they were believed to exist at all. In my experience, when one reports on such schools, educators have tended to regard the information as anecdotal, and have tended to regard anecdotal data as inconsequential, atypical, and non-replicable.

The traditional professional forecasts for most low achievers has been that they would remain so. In fact the low achievement has often been taken as a certain indicator of low intellectual capacity. The basic assumptions of current assessment practice make this definite, since the goal of present I.Q. based assessment is merely to **find** or **to identify** students according to ''potential'' so that they may be placed in known tracks where certain outcomes are expected.[2]

Research in education has been focused effectively on teaching only during a very recent period, much of it coming in the 1970s and 1980s. We have tended to look for learner traits or characteristics, family SES background variables, and racial or cultural differences in intellect to explain variation in achievement. Moreover, we have selected the function of **prediction** as the highest work for professional educational psychologists. It may be no exaggeration at all to say employers expect little else from school psychology other than I.Q. forecasting for placement in the right track.

Both teaching and testing are under attach. In both cases, the validity of what is offered claims the attention of the attackers. If either or both are invalid, then the relationship between them can be nothing other than invalid. There is a body of literature on testing and a body of literature on teaching as well, as a body of literature on students. However, there is not much, if anything, on the **nature** of the dynamic interaction between them. For example, Snow and Cronbach's ''aptitude treatment'' interaction is merely an attempt to describe the statistical relationships among essentially static measures of ''aptitude'' and ''treatment.''

The history of testing in education has been the history of the analysis of static evidence or data. In fact, the critical weakness of the use of I.Q. testing in schools is less with the popularly discussed questions of cultural bias and predictive validity than with the simple fact there is **not a shred of**

---

[1]Hilliard, A.G. ''Standard Testing and Non-Standard Population.'' *The Generator* (American Education Research Association, Division G), 11, 2, pp. 13-28.

[2]Hilliard, A.G *''Beyond Larry P.''* Keynote Presentation, Meeting of the Georgia Association of School Psychologists and the South Carolina Association of School Psychologists, Augusta, Georgia, 1982.

emipirical evidence that the predictive function itself, based on an attempt to do a global ranking of students by intellect, serves any valid pedagogical function at all. In other words, there are no data to show that teaching or learning are improved as a consequence of the use of I.Q. tests.

Under the present system of I.Q. test use in the schools, we look at a static measure of what is supposed to be intellect, and compare the results to a static measure of achievement. We do not know what happens in between. We are organized and predisposed to see **answers** to questions. We are set up to treat a given answer as if it has the same meaning for each respondent. Our present system of testing yields no important knowledge of the learning process and no knowledge of the teaching treatment. We know the answers which are given, but dc not know what is behind the answers. Therefore, test givers are not in a position to help teachers to know how to respond to what is behind them.

One of the things which is behind a given answer is the presence or absence of some generic skills or thinking conventions which may, with appropriate mediation be acquired by a student, as a language. When neither student nor teacher understands that there is something behind the answers, or more precisely what is behind them, the failure of a student to learn will produce frustration, hopelessness, despair, withdrawal, defensiveness and so forth.

In short, appropriate teaching must be addressed to what is **in between** the mythical "intellect" and student achievement. Further, appropriate teaching is valid teaching. Reuven Feuerstein's **Learning Potential Assessment Device** (LPAD) and **Instrumental Enrichment** (IE) system is, to my knowledge, the only "game in town" at present) not that it has exhausted all the possibilities by any means.[3] However, it has a theory of learning, a theory of teaching, validated strategies for teaching which flow from the theories and academic achievement results to show for it.

I make the assumption that learners learn best when they are able to see what is going on. Precision feedback from a supportive teacher helps this to happen. teachers ultimately are unique individuals who teach a number of unique individuals, not statistical abstractions. Carl Jung[4] has explicated this elegantly.

> The statistical method shows the facts in the light of the ideal average but does not give us a picture of their empirical reality. While reflecting an indisputable aspect of reality, it can falsify the actual truth in a most misleading way. This is particularly

---

[3]Feuerstein, R. *Instrumental Enrichment*. Baltimore: University Park Press, 1980.
[4]Jung, C.J. *The Undiscovered Self*. New York: Mentor, 1958, p. 17

true of theories which are based on statistics. The distinctive thing about real facts, however, is their individuality. Not to put too fine a point on it, one could say that the real picture consists of nothing but exceptions to the rule, and that, in consequence, absolute reality has predominantly the character of irregularity.

[In the statistical world], Judged scientifically, the individual is nothing but a unit which repeats itself ad infinitum and could just as well be designated with a letter of the alphabet. For understanding, on the other hand, it is just the unique individual human being who, when stripped of all those conformities and regularities so dear to the heart of the scientist, is the supreme and only real object of investigation. The doctor, above all, should be aware of this contradiction. On the one hand, he is equipped with the statistical truths of his scientific training, and on the other, he is faced with the task of treating a sick person who, especially in the case of psychic suffering, requires **individual understanding**. The more schematic the treatments, the more resistances it — quite rightly calls up in the patient, and the more the cure is jeopardized. The psychotherapist sees himself compelled, willy nilly, to regard the individuality of the patient as an essential fact in the picture and to arrange his methods of treatment accordingly. Today, over the whole field of medicine, it is recognized that the task of the doctor consists of treating the sick person, not an abstract illness.[5]

The impact of the use of present tools and paradigms in testing in particular and teaching in general, is to supress evidence of dynamism and uniqueness. The **dynamism** in cognition means that the process occurs **within** an individual and not according to an external model of abstract average content and timing; **and** further, it occurs as an **aspect** of an **interactive** student-teacher-context process. The existence of unique patterns of interactive dynamism, is the reality confronted by the teacher, not the stasis suggested by our previous paradigms. For example, the popular factor from I.Q. tests called "g" is the end product of testing. But, what does the knowledge of this mysterious "g" enable a teacher or psychologist to do to improve instruction?

Key Features

The LPAD/IE system rectifies previous testing/teaching problems. It moves forward not from the **inference** of cognitive functions or from the inference of a single global function, but from the **observation** of functions. The observed functions can be anticipated because of the clinically derived cognitive map, and in particular, that portion of the cognitive map which details the specific "deficient cognitive functions" to be sought in the three phases of the cognitive act.

The LPAD/IE system does not rely upon labels for categories of learners, nor does it rely upon any consideration of etiology, since the cause of a specific deficiency will in no way modify the strategy for assessment or teaching. In all cases, the assessor/teacher begins work with what is

---

[5]*Ibid.*, pp. 17-20.

available in cognition and moves to produce what is not by all means necessary. With the LPAD/IE system, **process, treatment**, and the **relationship** between them are explicit and are validly linked.

The LPAD/IE system is one where the assessor knows where he or she is going (because of the cognitive map), and how he or she intends to get there. Perhaps most important of all is that there is somewhere to go. This system uses several tests which we have come to thing of as "standardized" tests of mentality. Yet, they are used in non-standard (in the traditional sense) ways. To be more accurate, they are used with a standard **approach**, but not for the purpose of the quantification of ranks for students. They are used to set up the strategies for precision remedial teaching. In this system the true "instrument" is the assessor, not the test, which no longer does most of the thinking **for** the psychologist. Skilled professional judgment and actions are the central core of the whole thing.

It is to the everlasting credit of Feuerstein and his associates, that they have not fallen for the temptation to close the system. Feuerstein himself has emphasized the LPAD/IE approach is **not** buried in particular instruments. Further, he has suggested the the list of deficient functions is tentative, approximate, and incomplete. It is the approach which is central. Parts of it which interest me most are as follows:

(1). Cause the learner to expose his/her learning processes.
(2). Analyze what is exposed by means of the cognitive map.
(3). Get learner to see the process and to evaluate the impact of changes in it. (insight)
(4) Precision mediation is initiated to modify cognitive structures.

Feuerstein and his associates do not accept the idea that there are "critical periods" for cognitive development. This theory comes from studies of imprinting in birds. His clinical results and those of others appear to bear him out.

The LPAD/IE system is based on a way of thinking not **the** way to think. In my own formulation from previous research[6] (Hilliard, 1976), and in the work of others, poles of behavioral style and cognition are described. I think of analytic/objective and synthetic/personal poles which are similar to Cohen's[7] (1971) analytic and relational, Shapiro's[8] (1965) obsessive, com-

[6]Hilliard, A.G. *"Alternatives to I.Q. Testing: An Approach to the Identification of Gifted Minority Students."* Final Report, Special Education Support Unit, California State Department of Education, ERIC — ED 147 009, 1976.
[7]Cohen, R. *"The Influence of Conceptual Rule Sets on Measures of Learning Ability."* Race and Intelligence. Anthropological Association, 1971.
[8]Shapiro, D. *Neurotic Styles.* New York: Basic Books, 1965.

pulsive and hysterical, Witkin[9] (1954) field independent and field dependent, and Oinstein's left-brain and right-brain notions, among others. In my opinion, some of the "deficient functions" are true deficiencies which may, for example, be organic in origin. In other cases, what may appear to be "deficient functions," are merely alternative styles of precessing information which have their value in certain settings. For example, too much rigor in explicitness may well impede the function of "sizing up" a whole situatiuon. (Cohen, 1971). In fact the "efficient" cognitive functions may be "deficient" in certain settings. Typical school settings place a high value on precision, conformity to specific conventions, a narrow focus on types of information, and a full explication of what is known. The LPAD/IE system is superior in the development of cognitive structures for this pole of the cognitive continuum, and for the remediation of problems which occur in learners due to some deep deficiency at that pole. Much more work must be done to deal with thinking at the other pole.

Implications

The Feuerstein LPAD/IE system stands in the same relationship to pedagogical strategy as Piagetian formulations did previously to educational theory, or at least to cognitive theory. In a discipline that was theory poor at the time, Piaget rescued professionals from problems of credibility and legitimacy, to the extent that his though dominates the field of education and cognitive psychology today. One the system is broadly understood, it could become **the** system in the eyes of a strategy anemic profession. This can be both good and bad. But I will say more about that later.

The LPAD/IE system can restore some of the life and excitement to education which has declined in the face of a stultifying mechanism in the classroom and school since it has much to offer to teaching as to testing, to the teacher as to the testor. Testing practice will be improved, the communication between assessors and teachers will be more validly grounded, and above all, the LPAD/IE principles are generic to pedagogy. Helping teachers to develop a more sophisticated process for the analysis of the teaching and learning interaction, irrespective of content, can do nothing but good. The general level of professional dialogue would be raided by a quantum leap if LPAD/IE principles were understood. Moreover, as I have observed, the human quality of the teaching/learning interaction would also be improved.

A shift from traditional assessment to LPAD/IE is much more than a shift from one type of test to an alternative. It is a shift from a whole system

---

[9]Witkin, H.A., et al *Personality through Perception: An Experimental and Clinical Study.* New York: Harper and Row, 1954.

of thought and assumptions. This has major implications for training, retraining, and administrative structures in schools. Job descriptions, categorical, placement, methods of funding support services, goals for instruction will all be affected drastically.

A real danger exists as this better system, in my opinion, is implemented. We have taught the profession and the general public to believe in the old categories and in the static nature of learner capacity. Now, we have no way of supporting a system which is built on opposite conceptions. How do we pay for remedial services if there are no categories of learners. Heretofore, we have tied our funding to individual clients by our estimate of the number of clients who bear a general label (gifted, average, or retarded) all the time. What we need here instead is a way of tying services to specific difficulties, with some estimate of their incidence, which is independent of **individual** learners, since we expect that many learners will only be temporarily in need of remedial services. Even "average" or gifted learners may benefit from some of the same services.

The adoption of an LPAD/IE approach must be followed by a massive inservice and public information effort. Otherwise, the LPAD/IE system will be seen merely as an alternative way of ranking by intellect for permanent placement in a category.

We must be prepared to expect some misuses of LPAD/IE systems. Among the potential misuses which I can anticipate are these. There will be a tendency toward a mystification of the process once a corps of trained assessors exist. This will flow from the natural tendency of some people to protect themselves from competition to to elevate their status by cloaking what they do in mysteries and codes. There may also be a tendency to bring stasis thought to dynamic assessment, causing atropy in the process. This may be accomplished by viewing structures as permanent and by initiating attempts to focus on comparative ranking of individuals by the perceived permanent structures. The first symptom of this will be when the push to **score** the LPAD or IE begins to emerge. Finally, because of the excellent highly developed approach to the assessment of cognition primarily on one end of a cognitive continuum, there will be a tendency to treat that pole as the whole of cognition and to ignore other aspects of the reality of human capacity which is merely extended and not deficient.

Those who philosophy and theory excludes a knowledge of culture and its normal variations will be unable to use the LPAD/IE systems properly, since such philosophies and theories also exclude the concept of intellectual change.

Conclusion

Psychologists and educators, special and regular, will owe a debt of gratitude to Feuerstein and his associates. They have provided the basis for a fundamental, valid, and vital shift in thinking and in practice.

Contributors

JOSEPH A. BALDWIN, Ph.D., Professor of Psychology and Chairman of the Psychology Department, Florida A and M University.

BEVERLY P. COLE, Ph.D., National Director of Education for the National Association for the Advancement of Colored People.

HAROLD E. DENT, Ph.D., Vice-President of Psychological and Human Resources Consultants, Inc., (Berkeley, California) and Chairman of the Committee on Testing for the Association of Black Psychologists.

INGRID L. DRAPER, M.Ed., Executive Director, Office of Special Education, Detroit Public Schools.

ALEATHA C. HAMILTON, M.Ed., Administrative Assistant, Office of Special Education, Detroit Public Schools.

PATRICIA HEASTON, Ph.D., Director of the Bureau of Child Study and Psychological Services, Chicago Public Schools.

ASA G. HILLIARD, III, Ed.D., Fuller E. Callaway Professor of Education, Georgia State University.

MARY R. HOOVER, Ph.D., Dean of Graduate Studies, Delaware State College.

JANET JONES, M.Ed., Staff Development Specialist, Office of Special Education, Detroit Public Schools.

DORIAN LATHAM LEE, M.S., Graduate Assistant, Howard University.

ARMANDO M. MENDOCAL, III, Public Advocates, Inc..

WADE NOBLES, Ph.D., Executive Director, Institute for The Advanced Study of Black Family Life and Culture, Incorporated (Oakland, California) and Associate Professor of Black Studies, San Francisco State University.

W. D. PIERCE, Ph.D., Clinical Psychologist, San Francisco, California.

ROBERT L. POLITZER, Ph.D., Professor of Education and Counseling, Stanford University

ALICE M. SCALES, Ed.D., Associate Professor of Education, Department of Instruction and Learning, School of Education, University of Pittsburgh.

ORLANDO L. TAYLOR, Ph.D., Dean of the School of Communications and Graduate Professor of Communication Sciences, Howard University.

JOHN G. WEISS, M.A., Founding Executive Director of the National Center for Fair and Open Testing and Executive Director of FAIRTEST, Cambridge, Massachusetts.

G. I. WEST, Ph.D., Professor of Education in Counseling, San Francisco State University.